The
Flaming Sword

Tai Ikomi

PNEUMA LIFE

PUBLISHING

The Flaming Sword

Tai Ikomi

Unless otherwise noted, Scripture quotations are taken from the New King James Version. Copyright 1979, 1980, 1982, Thomas Nelson Inc., Publishers. Scriptures marked KJV are taken from the King James Version of the Bible.

Printed in the United States of America
ISBN: 1-56229-414-8

Pneuma Life Publishing
P. O. Box 10612
Bakersfield, CA 93389.
(805) 324-1741

Contents

Foreword
Introduction

Foreword

In the midst of a national crisis in which homes disintegrate, youth lack moral guidance, and the church seems unable to stem the tide of evil in our society, Tai Ikomi's book offers hope. Because the Word of God stands forever, it brings an expectation to those who read, memorize, and meditate on its many unshakable promises. This book will spark the flame of love for God's Word afresh and anew in many hearts.

Tai's expert method of teaching the reader to memorize Scripture helps new believers retain truth and challenges even seasoned ministers of the gospel. As a pastor/teacher, I recommend this invaluable volume to every believer. I even require it for every minister at Rose of Sharon Ministries. As Tai's pastor, I wholeheartedly recommend this book to every person who wants to stand firm in Jesus Christ.

Dr. Elizabeth Hairston
Pastor/Founder
Rose Of Sharon Ministries
Founder
Women With A Call International

Introduction

The Bible does not merely encourage Scripture memorization, it actually commands it. "And these words which I command you today shall be in your heart" (Deut. 6:6). Scripture memorization is, therefore, a divine mandate. Ever since giving the law to Moses, God commanded the Israelites to hide the written Word in their hearts.

The New Testament also emphasizes the primary place of the Word of God in the life of the believer. Jesus highly regarded the written Word of God and used it often: in His temptation, teaching, defense of His Messiahship, prayer to the Father, on the Cross, and after the resurrection. The Word of God resounded in the life of our Lord.

The Word of God continues to hold its power. Its efficacy to impart the life of God to the reader has not diminished. If you want to experience the life of God to a higher degree, let the Word of Life fill your thoughts. If you want to sense the presence of Jesus Christ, the Incarnate Word, then fill your inner being with the written Word. If you want to know the nearness of the Holy Spirit, then allow the Spirit-inspired Word of God to dwell richly in you. The power of the Word of God in the hearts of men has not diminished.

Those who have committed Scripture to memory can attest to the anointing of the Spirit of God in their hearts. It is not only the path that initiates us into God; it is also the path that leads us to great heights in God.

Dawson Trotman, founder of the Navigators, probably inspired more people to memorize Scripture than anyone in our century. He remarked: "Nothing pays higher dividends, for the time invested, than writing God's words on the tablets of our heart."

Tim LaHaye, a popular Christian author, wrote, "I have seen many individuals take giant spiritual steps as soon as they started memorizing Scripture." Mark Littleton echoes that thought: "Memorizing God's Word is critical to our spiritual growth." David, the man after God's own heart, also discovered the power of committing Scripture to memory.

The purpose of this book goes beyond simply motivating you to commit Scripture to memory. I want to show you the many benefits of Scripture memorization. First, it enables us to retain the Word of God in our minds. Second, it helps us to meditate on the Word. Third, the inherent power of God's Word transforms us as we memorize and meditate on it. The last two points show that Scripture memorization is not an end in itself but a means to an end.

I pray this book will open the eyes of believers to the many reasons for allowing his or her mind to be saturated with the Word of God. May you be spurred on to memorizing Scripture and enjoying its marvelous benefits!

1

How the Flaming Sword Works

The Word of God in our hearts is like a flaming sword that shields us from intruders. In the same way that God entrusted Adam and Eve to till and keep the Garden of Eden, God entrusts us with our hearts. The state of our heart, which determines our relationship with God, is our responsibility.

For example, we love God with our heart. With our heart we forgive or don't forgive our fellow man. With our heart we believe God or doubt Him. Without a pure heart, no one can walk with God. We must guard our hearts, for a lot depends on it. God has entrusted this domain to us, and we must be diligent to till and keep it.

After Adam and Eve sinned, God banished them from the garden. He placed a flaming sword outside its entrance to ward off all intruders. "So He drove out the man; and He placed cherubim at the east of the garden of Eden, and a flaming sword which turned every way, to guard the way to the tree of life" (Gen. 3:24).

The Word of God is a sword (Eph. 6:17). Hebrews 4:12 declares that the Word of God is sharper than any two-edged sword. The apostle John, when he saw the Lord Jesus Christ in His glorified state, noticed a sharp two-edged sword proceeding from His mouth (Rev. 1:16). Later, in the same book, John saw the Lord using that same sharp sword to attack His enemies (Rev. 19:15).

The Bible also calls the Word of God a fire (Jer. 23:29). The Word of God has gone through the furnace of God (Psalm 12:6). So the Word of God is both a fire and a sword. The Word of God is thus a Flaming Sword that proceeds from the mouth of God.

Into the Battle

This Flaming Sword is very powerful. It will attack any negative influence that wants to settle in your heart. If worldliness seeks to entangle your heart, the Flaming Sword that you have put in your heart and spoken with your mouth will go in every direction to attack it.

The Word of God, as the Flaming Sword, will attack the unforgiveness in your heart. It will quench that jealous spirit within your heart. It will fight depression; it will cut asunder the lust that has ruled you all these years. It will help you to conquer the sins that so easily beset you.

The Flaming Sword will banish the unwelcome guest of doubt from your heart. Many Christians want to believe God, but, for some reason, doubt seems to assail them. With the presence of God's Word, doubt is destroyed as faith enters. There is nothing the Flaming Sword cannot cut asunder.

It is natural for the Word to battle for you. The battle is not yours. Your part is to cultivate an obedient heart and allow the Word to dwell in you.

The more I memorize Scripture, on an average of one or two hours a day, the less I am moved by circumstances. The unseen Flaming Sword fights on my behalf. Hurts do not come easily, but if they do, they do not last long. If I find myself lagging in Scripture memorization, which happens once in a while, I fall prey to my circumstances. That's why I take Scripture memorization so seriously. The devil, of course, will seek to discourage you. *Do not allow him to!* A lot depends on your decision.

Breaks the Spirit of Fear

Fear stifles many people from living full lives. In fact, some people know nothing but fear. Fear has become a permanent resident in their hearts, and they seem unable to combat it. Fear overwhelms them for no obvious reason, causing their hearts to palpitate with anxiety and dread.

Various circumstances generate fear in many hearts. Some people are afraid of heights or crowds. A bad experience with a dog may cause a fear of animals. Loss of a friend may result in a fear of death. Doctors, counselors, and families try to help but are unable to dispel this fear in the hearts of their loved ones.

If, however, you allow the Flaming Sword of the Holy Spirit to stand at the entrance of your heart, it will destroy fear. Unhealthy fear is a spirit, and the presence of the Word of God will destroy it. When the heart overflows with the Word of

God, fear *cannot* stay. It can no longer dwell where the fire of the Word also burns. "Is not My word like a fire, saith the Lord; and like a hammer that breaks the rock in pieces?" (Jer. 23:29, KJV)

As the heart is filled more and more with the presence of the Word of God, the Christian will find, to his delight, that unwelcome guests have packed their bags and left. The Word of God breaks the rock of fear into pieces. It prevailed for many in the past, and it will prevail for you. The Word of God has not lost its power. Praise the Lord!

Delivers from Torment

Some Christians continue to be tormented from the spiritual and physical worlds. Bad dreams disturb their sleep, and they have nowhere to turn. They ask for prayer but experience no lasting results. Some secure temporary release but soon relapse to their former state.

At one time in my life, an unseen force oppressed me. Lying in bed, I would feel a hand pressing me down until I became uncomfortable. Whenever this happened, I called upon the name of Jesus. The hand lifted, and I felt a release.

Then I discovered the power of memorization. I began to memorize Scripture on a daily basis. I was not even conscious of its effect on me, but one day I realized I had not been attacked in a long time. The abundance of God's Word in my heart set me free!

The Syro-Phoenician woman came to Jesus, asking Him to cast an unclean spirit out of her daughter. The child was not present. Since the Word of God is not limited by distance,

Jesus spoke the Word in faith to deliver her daughter. Scripture says, "And when she had come to her house, she found the demon gone out, and her daughter lying on the bed" (Mark 7:30).

As a man of authority, the centurion knew the power of words. He said to Jesus, "Lord, I am not worthy that You should come under my roof. But only speak a word, and my servant will be healed. For I also am a man under authority, having soldiers under me. And I say to this one, 'Go,' and he goes; and to another, 'Come,' and he comes; and to my servant, 'Do this,' and he does it" (Matt. 8:8,9). Impressed with the faith that this Gentile exhibited, Jesus spoke the word, and the servant was made whole that same hour.

In other instances, the demon-possessed were present. Jesus spoke to the demons and cast them out. "So they were all amazed and spoke among themselves, saying, What a word this is! For with authority and power He commands the unclean spirits, and they come out" (Luke 4:36). The power of Jesus' spoken word delivered the oppressed.

The same mighty words are available to us. God has bequeathed this legacy to the church, to be used for His glory.

Do bad dreams disturb your sleep? Does the power of the devil hinder your walk with God? Do you experience hallucinations? Perhaps you are emotionally distraught and depend on pills to get through the day. Have you received prayer from great men of God without experiencing lasting change? Whatever your bondage, I have good news for you. Scripture says, "The entrance of your words gives light; it gives understanding to the simple" (Psalm 119:130).

When the Word of God abounds in your heart, the works of darkness cannot stay. Light and darkness cannot co-exist. Darkness must give way to light. Allow the Word of God to dwell in you, and the truth will set you free. "And ye shall know the truth, and the truth shall make you free" (John 8:32, KJV).

Purifies Our Hearts

Christians often associate the Word of God with gaining knowledge. Yes, the Bible tells us who God is and who we are. It also gives us insight into the spiritual and physical world. But that's not all. The Word of God not only imparts knowledge; it also imparts power.

When the Word of God richly dwells in our hearts, we expose ourselves to the power of God's Word. The innate properties of the Word of God have transformed lives for centuries — and still change men and women today. A regenerated heart receives continual cleansing as it comes in contact with the Word of God.

Jesus said, "You are already clean because of the word which I have spoken to you" (John 15:3). Then He turned to His Father and prayed, "Sanctify them through thy truth: thy word is truth" (John 17:17, KJV).

Later, the apostle Paul reiterated the means by which the Church is cleansed. "That He might sanctify and cleanse it [the Church] with the washing of water by the word" (Eph. 5:26). The Word of God is the instrument by which the Father and the Son cleanse the Church.

As you allow the Word of God to dwell abundantly in your heart, you are being purified by its cleansing properties.

We live in a polluted world. We bathe daily to remove the dirt and grime that we pick up simply by living. We still live in the flesh and among ungodly influence. When the Christian allows his heart to dwell richly on the Word of God, he will soon discover, to his delight, that sins are finding their way out.

When I memorize Scripture, I often find that my inward being undergoes a cleansing. I sense a holy environment around me, something akin to what I call "divine fragrance." I cannot define this atmosphere, except to say that I sense purity within. I feel this effect of the Word and allow it to stay on my heart through memorization. The Word of God is truly cleansing.

Conquers Wayward Thoughts

Many Christians struggle with bad thoughts. Try as they might to get rid of these evil thoughts, they fall short again and again. This is a sad reality. Lust, pride, jealousy, anger, and depression fill their hearts, even against their will. These believers have been cleansed and sanctified through faith in the blood of Christ, but, in reality, they continue to wrestle with impure thoughts. This is unwarranted and ought not to be. If only they would turn to the Word for adequate cleansing.

If you allow the Word of God to do battle for you, then victory is certain. The evil thoughts that have bound you will be cast down through the weapons of your warfare.

For the weapons of our warfare are not carnal but mighty in
God for pulling down strongholds, casting down arguments
and every high thing that exalts itself against the knowledge
of God, bringing every thought into captivity to the obedience of Christ (2 Cor. 10:4,5).

If you want your thoughts to be brought into the obedience
of Christ, use the spiritual weapon that God has placed at your
disposal. The sword of the Spirit, which is sharper than any
two-edged sword, will cut evil thoughts asunder.

For the Word of God is living and powerful, and sharper than
any two-edged sword, piercing even to the division of soul
and spirit, and of joints and marrow, and is a discerner of the
thoughts and intents of the heart (Heb. 4:12).

This weapon will cast down evil imaginations that dwell in
the thought realm. As you speak and meditate on the Word of
God through Scripture memorization, the inherent power of
the Word will war against the enemies of your soul.

God has not abandoned us. He has equipped us with
everything we need to live victoriously. He knows the battles
we constantly face. He has given us His Sword to do battle for
us. The devil cannot stand in the presence of the Flaming
Sword. Evil thoughts find their way out fast.

Constantly Cleanses

Do you want to be constantly cleansed? Let the Word of
God, the most powerful cleansing force ever known, richly
dwell in your heart. The entrance of the Word of God, the
Sword of the Spirit, brings light to dispel the works of
darkness. My own struggle with evil thoughts have been
solved through memorizing Scripture.

Let me share this example. The Lord had called me to do a job, and when I accomplished it, I felt a sense of unholy pride. Within minutes, I detected the presence of this stranger in my spirit. I could not get rid of this pride. I tried to be humble, but all my efforts proved futile. I did not know what to do. I tried praying, but this stubborn pride refused to budge.

Then I remembered the cleansing power of the Word. I began to memorize Scripture as fast as I could. Within a short time, perhaps less than five minutes, the pride dissipated. This is the reality of allowing the Word of God to abound in your heart. The more you grow in this process of memorization, the quicker your heart will respond.

A close friend of mine shared a similar testimony with me. She had problems with evil thoughts. Upon hearing me teach on the effect of the Word on the heart, she decided to memorize Scripture with renewed determination and faith. She found, to her delight, that all the evil thoughts simply vanished.

In 1985, five years after I began memorizing Scripture on a daily basis, I became charged with the fire of the Word of God. When it was time for Scripture memorization, my heart began to burn as the Word of God came in contact with it. Such was the effect of the Word on me after having committed almost a thousand verses to memory. Opening the Scriptures was like dropping a live coal on my heart. I could not take the fire of the Word. All I could do was weep before the Lord and worship Him as His presence surged through me. Years later, the Lord explained that He was cleansing me with the power of the Word of God.

2

Healing for Broken Hearts

The Word of God brings healing balm to the most shattered life. When a drunk driver killed my husband and three children, I was crushed. No words could penetrate my distraught heart. People offered their condolences. Family and friends tried to comfort me, but what could they say? No one could reach the recesses of my heart to remove the hurt. It cut too deeply. But when I turned to God, His Word became my refuge from the blast.

Thank God I had discovered the power of Scripture memorization years before my bereavement. It had been the source of my joy and satisfaction, and now — in my deepest agony and despair — I knew where to turn for comfort and relief. In my hour of need, the Word of God did not fail me.

Whenever my grieving heart groaned with sorrow, I rushed to the presence of God and poured it out. My parched soul absorbed the healing oil and wine that flowed from His presence. I began to memorize Scripture and found, to my delight, that God seemed to wash the sorrow, depression, and anguish from my system.

When my red, swollen eyes brimmed with tears, I knew the light of the Word of God would dispel the darkness that threatened to engulf me. His precious Word was one antidote that never failed me. I do not know what I would have done without the comfort and consolation of the Scriptures. I experienced, in an amazing way, that the Scriptures — though given through the instrumentality of man — are words of life and power from the God of heaven. He alone made us, and He alone can heal us no matter how deep-seated the wound.

Beauty for My Ashes

The Word of God spared me from insurmountable grief and brought emotional healing. It became the antidote to my depression during my bereavement. I could not afford *not* to memorize Scripture. Without the healing Word of God in my heart, I would have succumbed under the weight of incredible grief. Only those who have clung to the Scriptures in the midst of personal tragedy understand this. The strength of the Word of God saved me from emotional exhaustion. The Word of God healed my heart and bound up my wounds. When my consolers failed to reach the recesses of my heart, I knew the Word of God could.

After the release of my book, *His Beauty For My Ashes,* I began traveling to share with others the grace of God that sustained me during the loss of my husband and children. I emphasized Scripture memorization as a means to that grace. It burdened my heart to see precious children of God languish in grief. I offered them the same miracle ointment that I had applied to my own wound. I encouraged them to memorize Scripture and expose themselves to the power of the Word of God. I'm overjoyed to hear how they too have been blessed as they have committed Scripture to memory.

Scripture memorization enables the heart to dwell on the Word of God. During the process of memorization, a transformation occurs. The inherent power of God's Word works on the state of the heart. Let's examine some of the effects of the Word on the heart. The list, of course, is not exhaustive. No limitation can be placed on the Word of God, but exploring its life-changing power will encourage us to turn to Scripture with a new enthusiasm.

The Search for Emotional Healing

Some Christians have never had a healthy emotional life, and as such, have no point of reference. They may not realize that they need healing. Others once enjoyed a healthy emotional life, but something happened to destroy it. Childhood molestation, marital problems, rape, divorce, or death of a loved one have paralyzed the emotional stamina of many. No amount of therapy can bring total healing.

Many have depleted their finances in trying to find healing for their emotions, but all their efforts have proved futile. Resigned to misery, they assume they will be this way for the rest of their lives. This need not be the case.

The Word of God still heals. God has not withdrawn the power of His Word. "He sent His word and healed them, and delivered them from their destructions" (Psalm 107:20). The Word of God can relieve your emotional devastation. Scripture, the most effective balm known to man, will heal the most traumatic experiences and cleanse the deepest wounds.

Perhaps you have gone through a divorce. Divorce, which was never meant to occur, leaves its victims unstable and emotionally shattered. What used to be one, has been forcefully torn apart. It is against the law of nature. No human words can fully remove the pain and the ache.

Perhaps you are a widow or widower. The death of your spouse has created an aching void in your heart that no one can ever fill. Agony and despair engulf the joy you once shared with your spouse. Your world has fallen apart. Overwhelming loneliness weighs you down. You feel cheated, crushed, wounded, alone, and sad. Perhaps you have lost your zest for living. Total recovery seems beyond your reach.

God's Miracle Drug

Praise God, His Word is powerful enough to heal your heart. He will bind up wounds that refuse to heal. "He heals the brokenhearted and binds up their wounds" (Psalm 147:3). He continues to heal with His Word. The inherent power in God's Word goes forth unabated.

Saturate your heart with the Word of God; it is the miracle drug for your emotional disorder. It is the antidote to your emotional ailment. No depressant can come close to its effectiveness. No drug can heal like the Word of God. Antidepressants may have dangerous side effects, but the Word of God has none. It is whole. It is perfect. It proceeds from the God who made you. It is, therefore, compatible with your heart. By memorizing the Word of God, you begin to heal your emotions.

When the Word of God heals, no residue of the past remains. The Word will heal you totally and entirely. It knows no impossibilities. No matter how deep the wound, God's Word goes deeper still. The Word will reach the most hidden places. Yes, you can laugh again because the Word is healing your heart. A new world will be open to you — a world of tranquility and joy.

When depression knocks at the door, you know where to turn. Go to the Word that heals. The Incarnate Word, our Lord and Savior Jesus Christ, used the same word to heal the sick and bind up the brokenhearted. He has bequeathed to us the legacy of the Word. Let the same Word richly dwell in your heart. Let its healing power have its effect on your heart.

Replacing Depression with Joy

Another by-product of meditation is joy. The Word of God brings joy even in the midst of tribulation. Jeremiah experienced this phenomenon. "Your words were found, and I ate them, and Your word was to me the joy and rejoicing of my heart" (Jer. 15:16). Jeremiah found the book of the Law and chewed on it. In other words, he pondered it, meditated on it, and digested it. The Word stayed in His heart a long time, and he experienced the joy that comes from having a heart that overflows with Scripture.

David also experienced this. He wrote of a sweetness that accompanied meditation and led to gladness of heart. "My meditation of him shall be sweet: I will be glad in the Lord" (Psalm 104:34, KJV).

I have experienced this phenomenon again and again. The more I memorize Scripture, the more joyful I become. This joy is not dependent on circumstances but on the eternal Word that abides forever. Everything may be going wrong around me, but inside I'm rejoicing in God. A lasting joy — one that is not governed by or dependent on my fluctuating moods — can only be imparted by the Holy Spirit. I fight depression in my life through Scripture memorization.

The Bible talks of a joy in the presence of God (Psalm 16:11). The Word of God is God Himself (John 1:1). In the presence of the Word of God, there is joy. Great joy is attached to the Word of God. "The statutes of the Lord are right, rejoicing the heart" (Psalm 19:8, KJV). The Psalmist experienced the exuberance of God's Word when he wrote, "I rejoice at Your word as one who finds great treasure" (Psalm 119:162).

The thrill of winning first place or achieving a goal cannot compare with the joy of having God's Word in your heart. The former is short-lived; the latter is eternal and more fulfilling.

Friend, have you lost the joy of your salvation? Are you despondent? Have you tried to regain it but without results? Then go to the Word. Do not simply read it. Go a step further — meditate on it, ponder it. Like Jeremiah, David, and a host of other Christians, the words of the Lord will become the joy of your heart.

You will no longer need to depend on circumstances. Your joy will be based on the Word of God, which is the inheritance that our Father has given to us. The Psalmist declared, "Your testimonies I have taken as a heritage forever, for they are the rejoicing of my heart" (Psalm 119:111).

When the enemy uses circumstances to deprive you of your joy, you can run to the refuge of the Word of God. But do not wait for bad circumstances. Fill your heart with the heritage that God has given you. Make the Word of God your constant companion. Let it be your friend. It will not disappoint you.

Whenever I feel down, which is very rare now, I go to the Word and begin to memorize by speaking it out. The Word has never failed me. No matter how depressed I may be, the entrance of God's Word into my heart brings light. The longer I memorize God's Word, the easier it is for my heart to respond. Other things may fail, but the Word has never failed me.

Delighting in the Word

As you memorize and review your Scripture verses daily, your love for the Word of God begins to grow. You will find a delight in the Word that you never knew before. As your pleasure in the Word increases, Scripture begins to take precedence over other things in life.

The more you meditate, the greater the delight. Nothing can compare to the wealth of delight you have in the Word of God. The psalmist declared, "The law of Your mouth is better to me than thousands of shekels of gold and silver" (Psalm 119:72). Having delighted in Scripture, he couldn't compare all the riches in the world to the Word of God. He wrote, "More to be desired are they than gold, yea, than much fine gold; sweeter also than honey and the honeycomb" (Psalm 19:10).

David would rather choose the Word of God than millions of dollars, for the Word gave him greater satisfaction, fulfillment, and delight than all the wealth of the world. "How precious also are Your thoughts to me, O God! How great is the sum of them!" (Psalm 139:17)

No words can adequately describe the thoughts of God (God's Word) to the psalmist. He prayed for God to continue to teach him inwardly, for there he had found true delight. "Make me walk in the path of Your commandments, for I delight in it" (Psalm 119:35).

His delight in the Word of God saved him from an unpleasant situation. "Unless Your law had been my delight, I would then have perished in my affliction" (Psalm 119:92). Had he not discovered these delights, his unpleasant circumstance would have engulfed him. In the midst of it all, he could go to the Word of God, which had become his pleasure.

Job also delighted in the Word of God. "I have not departed from the commandment of His lips; I have treasured the words of His mouth more than my necessary food" (Job 23:12). The Word of God, which Job had esteemed and obviously pondered, delighted him more than his daily food. He would rather do without his food than go without the Word of God. The psalmist echoed this thought, noting that God's Word is "sweeter also than honey and the honeycomb" (Psalm 19:10).

How would you evaluate your love for the Word of God? Do you delight in the Word of God? Do you aspire after it? Then begin to memorize Scripture. As you do, your heart will begin to delight in the Word of God.

3

Memorizing Your Way to Spiritual Growth

Memorizing Scripture has a lasting effect on our entire spiritual life. Let's look at several ways that Scripture memorization helps us grow as believers.

God's Word Induces Prayer and Praise

Prayer is another outcome of memorization. During memorization, the tendency to breathe a word of prayer here and there is very strong. When a truth of the verse dawns on you, it is natural to simply get on your knees. You may find yourself praying that the truth might sink deeper in your heart. It can also lead you to a prayer of repentance as the Holy Spirit convicts you of a particular sin in your life.

Memorization and meditation often lead to offering a prayer of dedication. As the truth of the verse dawns on you, the tendency to look up to heaven and renew your dedication to God is strong. Since meditation is not superficial, it takes longer to search yourself before God and purpose to do all the Lord has commanded.

Meditation also enables you to pray for longer periods of time. Meditation on the Word enables you to enjoy the presence of God, and prayer is one facet of fellowship with God. Believers often cannot spend time in prayer because they lack delight in God. To them, prayer is a drudgery. After having tasted the joy, delight, and peace that characterizes the presence of God through meditation, prayer becomes more inviting. The desire for God's presence increases, and prayer inevitably lasts longer.

Praise also springs from meditation. A promise or a new insight may overwhelm you, prompting you to lift up your heart in praise and thanksgiving to the Almighty.

God's Word Produces Peace and Trust

The more you allow your mind to dwell on the Word, the greater peace you have. "Great peace have those who love Your law, and nothing causes them to stumble" (Psalm 119:165). Amidst the most trying circumstances, your peace will remain.

God Almighty promises to grant peace to those who allow their minds to stay on the Word of God. "You will keep him in perfect peace, whose mind is stayed on You, because he trusts in You" (Isaiah 26:3). This peace comes as a result of fixing one's mind on God's Word. As the truth of God's Word sinks deep in the heart, trust is born. Peace and trust go hand in hand.

As a result of your prolonged contact with the Word of God, your heart becomes established in the truth of God's Word. It becomes easier to trust God in this atmosphere of peace and serenity. You have an adamant faith in God to care for all your needs.

Jesus could sleep through the storm because He enjoyed the peace of God. The more you meditate on God's Word, the more peace and trust will rule your heart.

The Word of God is also a tranquilizer to calm the nerves. In an age of constant pressure and tension, the Word of God serves as the antidote to stress. When I feel the weight of pressure, I turn to the Word of God. Scripture memorization enables me to get up refreshed. I feel calm, renewed, and energized. Joy and peace envelope me like a blanket. It is as if I have been to heaven and back.

Remember that we are made by the Word of God, and only the Word of God can restore us. Try it —it works!

God's Word Yields Love

The love of God also increases, for your heart is being fashioned after God's own heart. The words of God are declared to be the thoughts of God to man (Psalm 33:11, KJV). With the thoughts of God in your heart, your heart takes on a new heart — the heart of God. You can have a heart patterned after God's heart because you have allowed your thoughts to be filled with His thoughts. Your heart begins to love what God loves and hate what God hates. His desires become your desires. His mind becomes your mind. Soon your heart begins to be heavenly minded. No longer will you need to force yourself to set your affection on things above. As a result of the prolonged contact of the Word with the heart, the heart continues to experience perfection.

Many Christians desire to be heavenly minded. They want to love God and their fellow man. They desire to think from a spiritual, not carnal, perspective, but they seem to fall short every time. God does not expect us to be heavenly minded on our own, for He knows our weaknesses.

If you allow the Word of God to dwell in your heart abundantly, you will begin to notice, to your delight, that your heart is tender toward God. Your heart is being patterned after God's heart. Your heart begins to desire the things of God. Soon, you may, in all humility, know that you are a man or woman after God's own heart.

Loving God results in loving your neighbor as well. Since God loves everyone, you too begin to experience the will to love others. I am not talking about a mere emotion. I refer to the will in your heart to love those who do not love you — the unlovely and the difficult. God will also enable you to love your brothers and sisters in Christ in the same way that Jesus loves the Church.

God's Word Builds Faith

The more you allow your heart to be filled with the Word of God, the more prepared it is to accept the Scriptures as true and reliable. One of the frustrations Christians experience is their seeming inability to have faith in God. They exert all their strength to trust God, but they are unable. They know intellectually that God can do all things. He is Jehovah-Jireh, the Provider of all good things. Their intellect understands it, but faith continues to elude them.

The Bible says that "faith comes by hearing, and hearing by the word of God" (Romans 10:17). God says so, and, of course, it is true. How then can we reconcile the fact that faith is not always produced even after exposing ourselves to the Word of God?

In the Parable of the Sower (Luke 8:4-15), Jesus pointed out that the fruition of the Word of God depended on the state of the heart. If the Word of God is planted on stony or thorny ground, it will not bring forth the fruit of faith, peace, grace, and so on. The state of the heart is the key to germinating the seed of the Word.

That same Word helps our heart to be good ground. Saturating your heart with the Word of God removes the weeds and thorns that hinder the germination of the Word. The Word of God produces faith, but only if it is sown on a "noble and good heart" (Luke 8:15).

If you want your heart to be that good ground, then immerse it in the Word of God day and night. The more you immerse your heart in the Word, the more noble it becomes. The more noble it becomes, the more it can germinate the seed of God's Word to faith.

God's Word Equips to Discern

The Word of God takes you into the thoughts of God. You know the thoughts of His heart through the Word He has given to humanity. As your heart meditates on the thoughts of God, you are better equipped to hear the heartbeat of God.

For example, for a computer disk to be able to receive information that can be translated into data, it must first be formatted. If it is not formatted, it cannot read information the computer attempts to transfer. Once it is formatted, it can take as much information as its capacity allows.

The same holds true in our hearts. When the Word of Christ dwells richly in us, we are formatting our hearts to be able to detect the Word of God. The apostle Paul commanded the Colossians, "Let the word of Christ dwell in you richly in all wisdom . . ." (Col. 3:16).

Since our hearts are accessible to voices other than the voice of God, care must be taken to train it. The heart must be taught to detect who is speaking. It must be equipped to discern the voice of the Shepherd — the Lord Jesus Christ.

As a young Christian, I was told I could hear the voice of God. I applied myself diligently to hear God's voice. Through experience I have learned to distinguish the voice of God from that of the devil or of my own mind. I have learned to compare what I hear with Scripture, and if what I hear is not based on the Word, I reject it — no matter how spiritual it sounds. God simply cannot change His Word. I appreciate my spiritual mentors for ingraining this truth in me.

The voice of God has proved invaluable in moments when I needed definite direction in my life. Life would be even more difficult at times, except for the fact that God often drops a specific word in my heart. Whenever I meditate on Scripture, I seem to hear the distinct voice of God all the more. The presence of the Word of God in my heart has proved to me to be a pathway to hearing the voice of God. Hallelujah!

God's Word Changes Circumstances

Another fascinating outcome of Scripture memorization is its effect on your circumstances. As you read Scripture aloud, you create a healthy aura around you. You speak forth words of life into your environment. Since the words of God are holy, you are creating holiness in your surroundings.

You may also begin to notice that if you displease the Lord, you may feel unholy inside as you begin to quote Scripture and meditate on it. Your heart is coming in contact with the Word, which is holy.

Ask the Lord to search you. If you already know what the sin is, do not spare yourself. Do not deceive yourself by asking the Lord to tell you again. If He has told you once, why ask again? Confess it, and ask the Lord to cleanse you from all unrighteousness. Continue to memorize Scripture, for in doing so, you continue to experience cleansing. Jesus told the disciples, "You are already clean because of the word which I have spoken to you" (John 15:3).

Since the words of God are powerful, the atmosphere around you imbibes the power of the Word of God. The Word of God must change the state of things that it touches. The Word of God has an unbroken record of being able to alter circumstances.

Our world was in chaos. It was without form until the Word of God was spoken into it. God spoke light to our world, and darkness vanished (Gen. 1:3). The effect of the Word of God is powerful. Out of a chaotic environment, our world could now boast of beauty. God Himself said that it was good.

The same Word of God continues to hold all things in order: "... and upholding all things by the word of His power, when He had by Himself purged our sins, sat down at the right hand of the Majesty on high" (Heb. 1:3).

The Word of God has an innate potency to effect a desirable change in your surroundings. To your delight, you find you can sense the presence of God around you. Wherever you go, the environment is charged with the Word of God.

When people come into contact with you, they may sense this unusual presence of God. The aura you carry is holy, emitting a degree of spiritual dignity and beauty.

Have you ever entered the presence of a great man or woman of God and, before you were introduced, you sensed something special about that person? It is the glory of the presence of the Almighty God.

While memorizing Scripture, I experienced the presence of God so strongly that I could not do anything but worship Almighty God. It seemed as if He came down by my side, and the words I was quoting were coming directly from His mouth. His presence was so close and so real that even if I left that location, I still carried that presence around. This was true in the life of Moses. God's glory shone on Moses' face because he had been with God.

Remember, the Word of God is God Himself. "In the beginning was the Word, and the Word was with God, and the Word was God" (John 1:1).

Much more can be said about the effect of memorizing Scripture. Experience it for yourself. Start memorizing three verses a week, with their references, and get ready to move to a spiritual dimension that only those who meditate on the Word of God are privileged to enjoy.

4

Out of Your Mouth and Into Your Heart

Christians often find it difficult to meditate on the Word of God. They protest that their mind simply wanders against their will. As they try to concentrate on the verse at hand, they are unable. Yet, Scripture commands us to meditate. In desperation, they give up hope. They feel this mental discipline is unattainable.

Some feel that meditation is for special Christians — ministers, full-time workers, or those who occupy a unique place in the kingdom of God. Others envy men of old, like David, who declared that he could meditate on God's Word day and night. The first book of Psalms describes a spiritually prosperous man who devoted his life to meditating on the Scriptures.

How can Scripture meditation be within the reach of every believer? Scripture memorization is the key that unlocks this discipline. It is difficult to memorize material without thinking of its content. The process of memorization leads to the ability to meditate. In the process of memorization, it is best to speak out the words. As you verbalize these words, a willing heart finds it easier to meditate on them.

The Link

The Lord reiterated this truth when He gave this command to Joshua: "This Book of the Law shall not depart from your mouth, but you shall meditate in it day and night, that you may observe to do according to all that is written in it. For then you will make your way prosperous, and then you will have good success" (Joshua 1:8).

God commands His words to be spoken. Our ability to speak sets us apart from the rest of God's creation. Speech and thought are interrelated. Our words affect the way we think, and what we think eventually shows up in our words.

The heart and the mouth are like twins. Our salvation is based on this concept. We must believe in our heart that God raised Christ from the dead and confess with our mouth that Jesus is Lord before we can experience the salvation of God (Romans 10:9,10).

At the onset of Joshua's ministry, God told him that the Book of the Law must not leave his mouth. How can we have the Word of God in our mouth all the time? Scripture memorization enables us to do this.

Speaking out the Scriptures naturally results in meditating on them. God also commanded Joshua: ". . . but thou shalt meditate therein day and night . . ." (KJV). David reiterated the same principle in his prayer, "Let the words of my mouth, and the meditation of my heart, be acceptable in thy sight . . ." (Psalm 19:14, KJV). David tied the words of his mouth to the meditation of his heart, for they are closely linked.

When God says something can be done, it means just that. God expects us to speak His Word and meditate on it day and night. Day and night is a figure of speech that denotes constancy. No day should pass without our practicing this discipline.

When you memorize Scripture, you will have the Word of God in your mouth and its meditation in your heart.

You and the Holy Spirit

When you memorize verses of Scripture and ponder them, the Holy Spirit becomes your private tutor. When you find yourself in the school of the Holy Spirit, He may stop you to impress the truth of a particular verse on your heart. The Holy Spirit, who inspired the Bible, begins to enlarge your understanding, making the truth of Scripture real to you. You'll begin to see things you never saw before as the Holy Spirit unlocks reality and life-changing truth.

As the Holy Spirit enlightens "the eyes of your understanding" (Eph. 1:18), you gain a deeper insight and understanding into the Bible. Christ promised He would impress the Word of God in our hearts. "But the Helper, the Holy Spirit, whom the Father will send in My name, He will teach you all things, and bring to your remembrance all things that I said to you" (John 14:26).

The more you allow the Holy Spirit to teach you, the more you are filled with Him. As you allow the Word of God to fill your heart, you begin to sense a sweet presence of the Holy Spirit. I have experienced this phenomenon through meditation. The power of the Word of God flows into your spirit. Because you are getting used to a greater degree of His presence, you can detect immediately when you grieve Him. You will be increasingly sensitive to anything that disrupts your relationship with God. A Christian who meditates on Scripture heads toward spiritual heights in God.

With the Holy Spirit as your personal teacher, you begin to gain a more correct grasp of the Word of God. Unbiased teaching comes directly from the revealed Word, and the Holy Spirit will not go against the Word. Your mind begins to shed traditional teaching that does not line up with the Word of God.

Although God has placed the ministry of teaching in the Church, the Bible also speaks of a teaching that comes as a result of the anointing of the Holy Spirit. "But the anointing which you have received from Him abides in you, and you do not need that anyone teach you; but as the same anointing teaches you concerning all things, and is true, and is not a lie, and just as it has taught you, you will abide in Him" (1 John 2:27).

A Desire to Obey God

Meditation on the Word of God also increases your desire to obey the Word. After the Lord commanded Joshua not to allow the Book of the Law to depart from his mouth but to meditate on it, He proceeded to explain why: ". . . that you may observe to do according to all that is written in it . . ."

When the Word of God dwells in the heart, obedience results. It is difficult to forget something that you meditate on all the time. Because your mind has dwelt so much on the Word of God, you will find yourself refusing to give in to opportunities to sin.

Suppose you have meditated on humility, and its truth has sunk deep in your heart. When the devil prompts you to exhibit pride, you recoil at the temptation. It is against something in your system. Your heart has been changed by the Word of God. You have tasted a higher life — a life of purity — for your heart has meditated on the Word. Little wonder the psalmist said, "Your word I have hidden in my heart, that I might not sin against You" (Psalm 119:11).

David, the man after God's own heart, did not depend on his emotional state to combat sin. Meditating on the Word of God enabled him to respect God's ordinances and decrees. "I will meditate on Your precepts, and contemplate Your ways" (Psalm 119:15). "I delight to do Your will, O my God, and Your law is within my heart" (Psalm 40:8). With the Word of God embedded in his heart, David desired to obey God.

Take time to memorize Scripture. It is a life-changing experience.

Benefits of Scripture Memorization

One benefit of Scripture memorization is the ability to quote the Word of God verbatim and from memory. Those who argue that Scripture memorization is not for everyone —

because not everyone is gifted to memorize — are themselves not given to Scripture memorization.

Your brain is an organ. Exercise it, and it will develop. Assuming that something is wrong will stop you from exercising your mind and subsequently deprive you of its growth.

Retaining memorized Scripture is very helpful for several reasons:

1. Provides Power to Witness

Scripture quotation is an invaluable witnessing tool. You may find yourself witnessing to a sinner to receive Christ. His eternal destiny is at stake. Paraphrasing a verse might alter the meaning of the verse. But when you have memorized the Scriptures verbatim, you are able to provide the sinner with correct information.

As a soul winner (every believer is called to this vocation), the Christian must be armed with adequate Scripture to lead a sinner to Christ. When you know Scripture, you exude confidence. You do not want to distract a sinner by your clumsiness in handling the Word of God. You should be ready with relevant information that they would need to yield their lives to Christ.

God may intervene and still save the sinner in spite of our lack of preparation, but isn't it better to fill our minds with the Word of God and make ourselves readily available to Him?

2. Builds Resistance Against Sin

Scripture memorization is also invaluable during the hour of temptation. Our Lord and Savior Jesus Christ left us an excellent example. Because Christ had committed Scripture to memory, He could draw on God's Word to fight the devil. Each time the devil tempted Him, the Lord responded with the Word that He undoubtedly had meditated on and had stored in His heart. On the three recorded occasions that the devil tempted Him, Jesus replied to the devil, "It is written . . ." (Matt. 4:4).

As Christians, we too must hide the Word of God in our heart. Reading the Word of God is good, but meditating on it helps you retain it and offers a much greater blessing.

Memorizing the Word builds your resistance against sin. As you allow the Word to dwell in you richly, you will begin to experience a strength against sin that simply transcends reason. The Word of God has an inherent power built into it.

Second, the Word of God helps you to know the mind of God on a particular subject. If the Word of God says lying is a sin, that knowledge helps you to avoid lying or deception — even if it will not "hurt anyone." It hurts you by jeopardizing your fellowship with God. As you mediate and ponder the Word of God, you will quickly notice the presence of sin in your life — and be prepared to overcome it.

3. Heals the Mind

When the devil attacks you with something that clearly is not God's will, you must keep on quoting the Word of God until a change occurs in your life.

Following the accident that took the lives of my family, my mind simply went berserk. Although I was still competent to put down my thoughts to a great extent, I could not verbalize them. My mind simply could not retain its train of thought, and I couldn't follow my thoughts to a logical conclusion. As a teacher, I wondered how I could teach when I could not even face two people and hold a logical discussion.

I tried everything, but nothing gave me a full recovery. Then I decided to try speaking forth the Word of God. I memorized this verse: "For God has not given us a spirit of fear, but of power and of love and of a sound mind" (2 Tim. 1:7). Then I repeated this verse dozens of times each day. Perhaps 15 times in the morning, 15 times in the afternoon, and 15 in the evening. After three weeks I found, to my delight, that I could carry on an intelligent conversation without feeling nervous. Praise God!

4. Comforts in Distress

Retaining Scripture also helps you to embrace its comfort. In times of despair and pain, you can draw from the wealth of verses you have stored up for yourself.

You remember Scriptures like, "Fear thou not; for I am with thee: be not dismayed; for I am thy God: I will strengthen thee; yea, I will help thee; yea, I will uphold thee with the right hand of my righteousness" (Isaiah 41:10, KJV). As you remember these words, you are able to fight the fear that threatens to overcome you.

The apostle Paul recommended that we comfort one another with the Scriptures (1 Thess. 4:18).

5. Refutes False Teaching

Retaining Scripture also helps you to defend the faith. The apostle Peter admonished us to "always be ready to give a defense to everyone who asks you a reason for the hope that is in you" (1 Peter 3:15). But how? We must be armed with what the Bible has to say about our faith. Both Peter and Paul used the Scriptures to defend their faith.

The early Church Fathers took Christianity from the jaws of Greek philosophers who wanted to merge Christianity with their philosophical tenets. The same weapon kept heretics from poisoning the Church.

Heretical teachings (false doctrines) have often tried to infiltrate the Church. In the early church, these false doctrines sounded reasonable and logical, but they came short of the written Word. A debate became inevitable between the heretics and the defenders of the faith. The believers didn't always have time to look up Bible verses. They often quoted Scripture from memory to refute these false doctrines. The future of the Church depended on the ability of the believers to protect the faith that was once delivered to the saints.

The same situation presents itself in our day. In an age characterized by excessive freedom of speech where false doctrines emerge at an alarming rate, we must know some Scripture from memory. Modern day humanism, the new age movement, psychic powers, and Islam challenge our faith. Not only is the battle to be fought from without, but also from within.

Even in Christian circles, you may hear a heretical teaching. It may be propagated by a well-known Christian leader, but, if it is opposed to the Bible, you must be able to defend the Word of God. Scripture memorization will aid you during these occasions. In fact, a similar challenge initiated me into Scripture memorization.

In 1980, I was leading worship in a Christian Student Fellowship in Grimsby, England, when an unexpected visitor came in. After the meeting, he objected that a woman had stood before the church to lead the singing. "Your place," he said, "is in the kitchen." My husband objected to this comment, as did the other brethren.

To refute this man's argument, we turned to the Scriptures, knowing that somewhere in Paul's epistles women were allowed to speak. Where, we did not know. We thumbed through page after page in the Bible looking for a defense for our belief. Unable to find the verse, we did what we could under such circumstances.

On our way home that evening, one of the brothers remarked that it was a shame we were unprepared for this visitor's challenge. What he said next altered the course of my Christian life. He pointed out that if it had been our academic work, we would have been more diligent and better prepared. That touched me. I knew I had to do something.

I purposed in my heart to start memorizing Bible verses and their references. I just knew that I must do it. And what a pleasant and life-changing task it has been!

I stumbled onto something that took me to great heights in God, shielded me against the storms of life, and became my city of refuge during the blast. My decision to memorize Scripture held my faculties together when I lost my husband

and three children. It also helped me, of course, in the defense of the gospel.

6. Combats Deception

I have never regretted my decision. Having decided to memorize Scripture, I began to write them down in a notebook. I memorized at home, on the bus, at work — anywhere and everywhere I could carry that notebook. Scripture memorization dominated my thinking. It became a consuming passion. Committing Scripture to memory has shielded me from heresies and voices that sounded like God's.

The devil may suggest a wonderful idea to you that sounds like the voice of God, but you can combat such subtle deception with the Word hidden in your heart. Do not take the retention of the Word of God lightly. It is important. It is the Sword of the Spirit against every temptation and heretical teaching. It prepares you for battle when you are suddenly called to speak up for your faith.

A Part of Your Life

The rewards of Scripture memorization cannot be confined to a book. God has given us the command to commit His Word to memory. He has a definite purpose in giving us this command. We must fill our hearts with the Word of God. It may not be easy at first, and it may look impossible. If we set our minds to it, we can accomplish this holy task. With the help of God, we can do all things through Christ who strengthens us.

Let Scripture memorization be a part of your life. When discouragement sets in, resolve to memorize Scripture. Expose yourself to the inherent power of the Word of God. Scripture is Spirit-filled, life-giving, and burning with the power of its Author — Almighty God.

As you move to a higher plane in your pursuit of the knowledge of Scripture, I pray your heart will experience the supernatural phenomenon reserved for those who allow the Word of God to dwell in their hearts richly. "Let the word of Christ dwell in you richly . . ." (Col. 3:16).

5

How To Memorize Scripture

Scripture memorization can be done in a variety of ways. Although the leading of the Holy Spirit is paramount, I will outline some general suggestions that I follow. I trust they will be helpful as you embark on hiding the Word of God in your heart.

1. Pray for Understanding

The first step to Scripture memorization is prayer. Without total dependence on the Holy Spirit, Scripture memorization is futile. The Holy Spirit will open your eyes to understand the Scriptures and to impart to you His presence.

After the resurrection Jesus not only expounded the Scriptures to His disciples, but He also opened their minds to grasp it. "He opened their understanding, that they might comprehend the Scriptures" (Luke 24:45).

Our prayer should be, "Open my eyes, that I may see wondrous things from Your law" (Psalm 119:18). Take time to pray for the presence of the Holy Spirit as you engage in this exercise. Do not hurry over this request. Reverently commit the session of Scripture memorization to the Holy Spirit. Be calm.

Before starting this session, determine how much time you will spend with Him. This way, you are not in a hurry to finish and leave.

2. Make it a Daily Exercise

Scripture memorization can be a daily exercise. After memorizing Scripture consistently, you will find it unthinkable not to memorize in a single day. But I do not advocate learning a new verse each day. I encourage beginners to start with three verses per week.

Sunday is a good day to start a new set of Bible verses. If you can, memorize three verses that day. If you cannot, start with one. Remember, the essence of Scripture memorization is not limited to retaining it immediately.

After memorizing three verses on Sunday, continue rehearsing them throughout the week. It's unlikely that you'll be able to quote them verbatim the first time you memorize them. Even when you think you know them, you may be unable to recall them two hours later. Do not be discouraged. This is normal.

When I memorize a new set of verses, I try to remind myself of them all day long — anywhere and everywhere. I try to remember them and speak them aloud even in the shower. Rehearsing them during my evening walk has blessed me tremendously.

I often sense the power of God as I recall His words. If I find myself unable to remember most of them, I simply go back to the Bible and start again. As I do that, I find myself meditating on them.

In the course of the week, as you rehearse Scripture over and over again, meditation becomes a natural by-product, retention begins to take place (even if it does not, do not worry), and you expose yourself to the inherent power of the Word.

3. Commit to a Certain Time Frame

Discipline is another integral part of this program. The devil will discourage you, for he knows the power of the Word. Resist his efforts at hindering you. The grace of God will help you, but your will must be present and you must persist.

Memorization, like prayer, is a discipline. But after a while, it becomes a pleasure. The same holds true for Scripture memorization. At times you may not feel like memorizing Scripture, but do it anyway. This is not a one-week commitment, but a life-long goal. Memorization and meditation lead to success in all areas of life.

Commit yourself to a certain time of day, and possibly a particular location, to memorize. I suggest 15 minutes a day for beginners. You may gradually increase to an hour. You may think you do not have time for Scripture memorization, but in most instances you do. It is a matter of priority. The more time I spend with God, the more time I have for other things.

While you attempt to memorize Scripture, the Holy Spirit may highlight a particular truth or lead you into prayer. This happens to me often. I may intend to memorize ten verses at a particular time, but I find myself able to master only two or three because of the enormous presence of the Holy Spirit. I just bask in His presence for the remainder of the time allocated to Scripture memorization. It is important to give the Holy Spirit the right of way.

You may also incorporate Scripture memorization into your quiet time. Select two or three verses from your daily reading and commit them to memory.

4. Repeat the Verse Out Loud

When you memorize, endeavor to say the verse out loud. When you meditate on them only in your heart, you deprive yourself of the benefits of speaking them into your environment. Moreover, when you read silently, you use only your eyes. When you verbalize Scripture, however, you also use your mouth and your ears.

Speaking out the words I memorize is much more spiritually refreshing than simply memorizing it in my heart. The extra effort pays great dividends.

Methods of Memorization

Now let's look at several methods of memorization. Once again, the leading of the Holy Spirit is very important. If you struggle with one method, try another. I'm sure you'll find a way to memorize that suits you best.

1. Topical Memorization

Beginners might want to start by memorizing verses according to different topics. Grace, faith, the Word of God, love, humility, holiness/sanctification, and repentance are good topics.

The advantage of the topical approach is that it enables you to accurately divide the Word of God. Memorizing topically allows you to see the importance the Bible gives each topic.

As you memorize Scripture on humility, you will understand the great importance God places on it. By the time you finish memorizing this topic, say 30 verses, God's Word will spur you to desire humility. This also makes you more conscious of your relationship with others in this regard.

By the time you finish studying topics such as holiness, grace, faith, love, covetousness, prosperity, and repentance, your mind is overwhelmed. Now you can accurately and intelligently divide these topics. You are able to accord each its importance. You know, for example, that love is greater than the gift of faith; justice and mercy, "the weightier matters of the law" (Matt. 23:23), are greater than prosperity.

Although the Bible is equally inspired, some doctrines are more important than others. That's why the apostle Paul accords love a greater place than the gift of faith. Scripture memorization is excellent for this demarcation.

Look through a concordance for a particular topic. Grace is one of my favorites. Not all Scripture on the topic needs to be memorized, but you should copy the references of some relevant verses. Then write down the verses in a notebook.

This process of writing begins to familiarize you with the verses.

You may use a computer to generate topical verses. Unfortunately, this method deprives you of writing the Word yourself and becoming familiar with it. A Bible software program may give you more Scripture than you want, and some of it might not be suitable for memorization.

What's the bottom line? Do what is best for you. I sometimes use a computer to generate verses. But if you're just starting to memorize on a daily basis, I believe it is more effective to use a concordance.

Writing these verses on 3 by 5 cards will enable you to carry them around. If possible, use different colored cards to differentiate your topics. This is suitable for verse by verse memorization but not for chapter memorization, which you should do directly from your Bible.

I prefer writing the verses in a notebook so I don't lose them. Of course, the disadvantage is its size. If you prefer, you may use both. But don't get too elaborate when writing down the verses and discourage yourself. Keep your method as simple as possible.

2. Chapter Memorization

Memorizing a chapter at a time may overwhelm a novice, but it's a good challenge for a more advanced student. You may decide to memorize three verses at a time until you complete the entire chapter.

Although I believe in the retention of Scripture, when it comes to chapter memorization, I do not place heavy emphasis on it. Remember that this discipline is not just to develop the ability to quote long passages from memory. Chapter memorization should emphasize meditation and the inherent power of the Word.

Because I have been practicing Scripture memorization for years, I can memorize a whole chapter in a day. Besides the richness I gain in meditation, I experience an overwhelming effect from the Word of God. The sweet anointing of the Holy Spirit is wonderful. I endeavor to retain chapters of the Word, but retention takes second place to meditation and the effect of the Word.

If God leads you to place equal emphasis on all aspects of memorization, feel free to do so. The best thing we can do is yield to the Lord.

3. Praise Memorization

The book of Psalms is invaluable in praise memorization. Memorizing praise verses or chapters enables you to praise God with the words He Himself inspired. Retention, in this instance, should be given equal place.

When I memorize praise chapters, I feel as if I am before the throne room of heaven. Giving God praise and adoration with His own words takes us to great heights in the Lord. God inhabits the praises of His children.

As you memorize these verses, you find yourself simultaneously praising God. After a while, you may use these verses to praise God in your devotions.

The chapters of praise I have memorized have proved invaluable to me during my quiet time. I may find myself often quoting (and meaning) four to five chapters of praise psalms at a time. It is a wonderful experience.

The book of Psalms offers many chapters that are ideal for memorization. Here are several good places to start: Psalm 95:1-7; Psalm 96; Psalm 98; Psalm 100; Psalm 145; Psalm 146; Psalm 147:1-11; Psalm 148; and Psalm 150.

4. Prayer Memorization

The Bible is filled with the prayers of godly men and women. If you have difficulty in your prayer life, try memorizing the prayers of the apostle Paul for the Church. Some of them are only two or three verses; others are much longer, such as Ephesians 1:17-23; 3:14-21; Philippians 1:9-11; and Colossians 1:9-12. This type of memorization naturally leads to prayer. You begin to know the will of God for your life while you simultaneously pray for it.

6

Questions and Answers About Memorization and Meditation

Q. What steps should I take to memorize Scripture?

A. Find a quiet location if possible. Determine how much time you want to spend memorizing Scripture. Don't set too lofty a goal and risk discouraging yourself at the outset. Stick to the time. Determine which method you will follow.

If you start with the topical program, selecting a relevant subject will help to motivate you. Do you need to learn more about God's love? Perhaps fear has been hindering you. Maybe you want to discover what the Bible has to say about witnessing. Get a concordance and scan the verses under a particular topic. Select the ones you want to memorize, and write down their references. Next, write them in a notebook or on index cards. Memorize as many as you need to gain a more comprehensive knowledge of the topic. This may take up to one month or more.

Q. I find it difficult to retain any information, so how can I memorize Scripture?

A. The brain is a muscle. If you exercise it, it will become stronger. You may not be able to retain many verses when you first start, but don't be discouraged. Keep at it. Little by little, you will be able to memorize more Scripture. Don't set an unrealistic goal for yourself. Do whatever you can, and expect God to bless it. Remember that retention is not all there is to memorizing Scripture. As you memorize Scripture, you are also meditating on it, which exposes you to the power of the Word of God.

Q. How can I find time to memorize Scripture with my busy schedule?

A. God is the Maker of time, but the devil is a time robber. As you honor God with your time, He will direct your affairs. When you give God time in memorization and meditation on His Word, He will weed out the unnecessary activities that deprive you of your time. Memorize Scripture for 15 minutes a day, then increase it as the Lord strengthens you.

Q. Being a student, I fear that memorizing Scripture might exhaust my mental faculties. What should I do?

A. Memorizing Scripture is a good diversion from your studies. You'll feel more relaxed when you return to your textbooks. Memorizing Scripture is not like preparing for an examination with all its pressure. If you start feeling pressure, you need to re-evaluate why you are memorizing Scripture. You should not try to impress anyone but God.

As a student, I memorized a lot of Scripture. Interestingly enough, I felt the discipline rejuvenated my thinking. My mind seemed to be able to take in more than it had previously. I cannot explain this phenomenon, but I have experienced it. I believe the inherent power of God's Word works on the mind as well as the spirit. This has been my experience, and it can be yours. Unless you try it, however, you may never know this dimension of the power of the Word of God.

Q. How much time should I spend on Scripture memorization each day?

A. Begin by spending at least 15 minutes in each session. As time passes, you may increase it to half an hour, then gradually to one hour. I advocate that a Christian should spend one hour each day in God's Word.

Q. If I can meditate silently on Scripture, why do I need to memorize it?

A. Meditation is not the only benefit that comes from memorizing Scripture. First, memorizing Scripture helps you to retain the Word of God for witnessing, combatting temptation, and ministering to others. Second, when you memorize Scripture — and speak it out loud — you create an environment around you that is charged with the presence of God.

When I feel lazy or physically exhausted, I resort to silent meditation. But I cannot wait until I am strong enough to speak out the verses. Nothing compares to speaking out the Word of God and enjoying more benefits of Scripture memorization. Remember that confession has a lot to do with our salvation, therefore, it is important. Indeed, our faith must be confessed in Jesus Christ before we are saved. We should not deprive ourselves of the benefits that come from verbally declaring the truth of God's Word.

Q. What Bible translation should I memorize?

A. I recommend the New King James Version, the Revised Standard Version, and the New American Standard Version. It is also a good idea to memorize from the Bible that you regularly study. I like the King James Version because it is poetic and therefore easier to retain. The chief disadvantage is that some words have changed in meaning since this version was first translated. Some modern translations, however, are rather difficult to retain for the same reason.

Q. Is it necessary to memorize the reference with the text?

A. It is a good discipline to do this since you may need to recall them when you minister to someone. Besides, it aids you in retaining Scripture by challenging your mind to perform at its best.

Q. Is it necessary to retain every verse I memorize?

A. It is important to retain some verses, especially in topical learning. You need not retain the references. If you can, great! If not, don't be discouraged. You will always need Scripture, so try to retain them.

Tim LaHaye, in his book, *How to Study the Scriptures,* offers this program for retaining Bible verses: If you review a particular verse daily for seven weeks, and once a week for seven months, and then once a month for seven months, you will remember it for the rest of your life. Endeavor to review some verses daily and some every week.

Q. How much time should I spend on a particular subject if I choose the topical program of memorization?

A. It depends on when you think you have memorized enough from a particular topic. After you move on to other areas, the Holy Spirit will eventually bring you back to earlier topics that you have memorized. Review them and try to add other verses to broaden your understanding.

Q. Is it better to write Scripture on index cards or in journals?

A. This depends on your preference. Index cards are more portable than a journal. The journal, however, enables you to see all the verses at a glance. Choose whatever suits you best, or use them both.

Q. Should I memorize Scripture to get an award in my church?

A. Yes, you may, but don't forget to memorize for your own personal enrichment. After all, why does the church offer awards for memorizing Scripture? It motivates you to hide the Word of God in your heart. That's the more important goal to pursue.

Q. If I finish memorizing my allotted Scripture verses before my time runs out, may I stop?

A. The emphasis is not on how many verses you are able to memorize, but on time spent with God. Some people may be able to memorize a verse in five minutes, while others need at least 20 minutes. While your mind may have grasped the Word, your heart might not have absorbed as much truth as it should imbibe. It takes time for the Word of God to work on your heart.

Q. I am a very busy person. Thinking of innovative ideas to increase productivity on my job consumes me — even after I leave work. I find it difficult to memorize Scripture without feeling that I am wasting time.

A. Even the busiest person needs a break to achieve maximum productivity. Your mind needs a diversion to function properly. You are not wasting time when you memorize Scripture.

When I was a student, and my mind was buried in my studies, I knew that memorizing Scripture relieved some of my mental burden. Because my business constantly demands my supervision and attention, I am sometimes tempted not to spend time in Scripture memorization. But I have learned not to give in to this temptation. I simply shut out everything and start memorizing. After memorizing Scripture, I feel rejuvenated and refreshed.

In the same way that God often multiplies my time, He will honor your step of faith in this area. Experiencing the peace of God is just one reward of Scripture memorization.

7

Scripture for Topical Memorization

A good way to start memorizing Scriptures is by topics. After memorizing 10-15 verses in a topic, I suggest you move to the next one. This gives you adequate information on the topic at hand, and going to other topics gives you a well-balanced view of the Word of God. The tendency to mishandle the Word of God is great when only one truth is emphasized at the expense of others. We must not fall into this error.

The topics in this chapter are by no means exhaustive, but they do give you a starting point. This section of the topical study is an excerpt from *The Believer's Topical Bible* compiled by Derwin Stewart. I suggest you get a copy of the book to benefit fully from it (For further information see the back of the book).

Who God Is

And we have known and believed the love that God has for us. God is love, and he who abides in love abides in God, and God in him (1 John 4:16).

God is Spirit, and those who worship Him must worship in spirit and truth (John 4:24).

Furthermore, we have had human fathers who corrected us, and we paid them respect. Shall we not much more readily be in subjection to the Father of spirits and live? (Heb. 12:9).

God is Sovereign and Omnipotent

Great is our Lord, and mighty in power; His understanding is infinite (Psalm 147:5).

"For My thoughts are not your thoughts, nor are your ways My ways," says the Lord. "For as the heavens are higher than the earth, so are My ways higher than your ways, and My thoughts than your thoughts" (Isaiah 55:8,9).

"Am I a God near at hand," says the Lord, "and not a God afar off? Can anyone hide himself in secret places, so I shall not see him?" says the Lord. "Do I not fill heaven and earth?" says the Lord (Jer. 23:23,24).

For with God nothing will be impossible (Luke 1:37).

Oh, the depth of the riches both of the wisdom and knowledge of God! How unsearchable are His judgments and His ways past finding out! (Romans 11:33).

Therefore, since we are receiving a kingdom which cannot be shaken, let us have grace, by which we may serve God acceptably with reverence and godly fear. For our God is a consuming fire (Heb. 12:28,29).

And I heard, as it were, the voice of a great multitude, as the sound of many waters and as the sound of mighty thunderings, saying, "Alleluia! For the Lord God Omnipotent reigns!" (Rev. 19:6).

God is the Creator of Mankind

Then God said, "Let Us make man in Our image, according to Our likeness; let them have dominion over the fish of the sea, over the birds of the air, and over the cattle, over all the earth and over every creeping thing that creeps on the earth" (Gen. 1:26).

So God created man in His own image; in the image of God He created him; male and female He created them (Gen. 1:27).

The burden of the word of the Lord against Israel. Thus says the Lord, who stretches out the heavens, lays the foundation of the earth, and forms the spirit of man within him (Zech. 12:1).

As you do not know what is the way of the wind, or how the bones grow in the womb of her who is with child, so you do not know the works of God who makes all things (Eccl. 11:5).

He has made the earth by His power, He has established the world by His wisdom, and has stretched out the heavens at His discretion (Jer. 10:12).

Trusting God

As for God, His way is perfect; the word of the Lord is proven; He is a shield to all who trust in Him (2 Samuel 22:31).

But let all those rejoice who put their trust in You; let them ever shout for joy, because You defend them; let those also who love Your name be joyful in You (Psalm 5:11).

And those who know Your name will put their trust in You; for You, Lord, have not forsaken those who seek You (Psalm 9:10).

Preserve me, O God, for in You I put my trust (Psalm 16:1).

The Lord is my rock and my fortress and my deliverer; my God, my strength, in whom I will trust; my shield and the horn of my salvation, my stronghold (Psalm 18:2).

As for God, His way is perfect; the word of the Lord is proven; He is a shield to all who trust in Him (Psalm 18:30).

Oh, taste and see that the Lord is good; blessed is the man who trusts in Him! (Psalm 34:8).

Whenever I am afraid, I will trust in You (Psalm 56:3).

Trust in Him at all times, you people; pour out your heart before Him; God is a refuge for us. Selah (Psalm 62:8).

I will say of the Lord, "He is my refuge and my fortress; my God, in Him I will trust (Psalm 91:2).

Trust in the Lord with all your heart, and lean not on your own understanding (Prov. 3:5).

Principles of Faith

So Jesus said to them, "Because of your unbelief; for assuredly, I say to you, if you have faith as a mustard seed, you will say to this mountain, 'Move from here to there,' and it will move; and nothing will be impossible for you" (Matt. 17:20).

For we walk by faith, not by sight (2 Cor. 5:7).

Let us hold fast the confession of our hope without wavering, for He who promised is faithful (Heb. 10:23).

Now faith is the substance of things hoped for, the evidence of things not seen (Heb. 11:1).

Whom having not seen you love. Though now you do not see Him, yet believing, you rejoice with joy inexpressible and full of glory (1 Peter 1:8).

Obedience to God's Will

For whoever does the will of God is My brother and My sister and mother (Mark 3:35).

And that servant who knew his master's will, and did not prepare himself or do according to his will, shall be beaten with many stripes (Luke 12:47).

If anyone wants to do His will, he shall know concerning the doctrine, whether it is from God or whether I speak on My own authority (John 7:17).

Above all, taking the shield of faith with which you will be able to quench all the fiery darts of the wicked one (Eph. 6:16).

For you have need of endurance, so that after you have done the will of God, you may receive the promise (Heb. 10:36).

And the world is passing away, and the lust of it; but he who does the will of God abides forever (1 John 2:17).

Praising God

I will praise the Lord according to His righteousness, and will sing praise to the name of the Lord Most High (Psalm 7:17).

The Lord is my strength and my shield; my heart trusted in Him, and I am helped; therefore my heart greatly rejoices, and with my song I will praise Him (Psalm 28:7).

And my tongue shall speak of Your righteousness and of Your praise all the day long (Psalm 35:28).

In God we boast all day long, and praise Your name forever. Selah (Psalm 44:8).

Great is the Lord, and greatly to be praised in the city of our God, in His holy mountain (Psalm 48:1).

My heart is steadfast, O God, my heart is steadfast; I will sing and give praise (Psalm 57:7).

Make a joyful shout to God, all the earth! Sing out the honor of His name; make His praise glorious (Psalm 66:1,2).

Let the peoples praise You, O God; let all the peoples praise You (Psalm 67:3).

I will praise You, O Lord my God, with all my heart, and I will glorify Your name forevermore (Psalm 86:12).

It is good to give thanks to the Lord, and to sing praises to Your name, O Most High; to declare Your lovingkindness in the morning, and Your faithfulness every night (Psalm 92:1,2).

Praise the Lord! Praise, O servants of the Lord, praise the name of the Lord! Blessed be the name of the Lord from this time forth and forevermore! (Psalm 113:1,2).

Great is the Lord, and greatly to be praised; and His greatness is unsearchable (Psalm 145:3).

Submitting to God's Will

He went a little farther and fell on His face, and prayed, saying, "O My Father, if it is possible, let this cup pass from Me; nevertheless, not as I will, but as You will" (Matt. 26:39).

Your kingdom come. Your will be done on earth as it is in heaven (Matt. 6:10).

Then He said to them all, "If anyone desires to come after Me, let him deny himself, and take up his cross daily, and follow Me" (Luke 9:23).

Who gave Himself for our sins, that He might deliver us from this present evil age, according to the will of our God and Father (Gal. 1:4).

For it is God who works in you both to will and to do for His good pleasure (Phil. 2:13).

For this is the will of God, your sanctification: that you should abstain from sexual immorality (1 Thess. 4:3).

Believing in Jesus Christ

Most assuredly, I say to you, he who believes in Me has everlasting life (John 6:47).

But as many as received Him, to them He gave the right to become children of God, even to those who believe in His name (John 1:12).

For God so loved the world that He gave His only begotten Son, that whoever believes in Him should not perish but have everlasting life (John 3:16).

He who believes in the Son has everlasting life; and he who does not believe the Son shall not see life, but the wrath of God abides on him (John 3:36).

Most assuredly, I say to you, he who hears My word and believes in Him who sent Me has everlasting life, and shall not come into judgment, but has passed from death into life (John 5:24).

Therefore I said to you that you will die in your sins; for if you do not believe that I am He, you will die in your sins (John 8:24).

But these are written that you may believe that Jesus is the Christ, the Son of God, and that believing you may have life in His name (John 20:31).

Sanctification

And you shall keep My statutes, and perform them: I am the Lord who sanctifies you (Levit. 20:8).

That I might be a minister of Jesus Christ to the Gentiles, ministering the gospel of God, that the offering of the Gentiles might be acceptable, sanctified by the Holy Spirit (Romans 15:16).

Now may the God of peace Himself sanctify you completely; and may your whole spirit, soul, and body be preserved blameless at the coming of our Lord Jesus Christ (1 Thess. 5:23).

But we are bound to give thanks to God always for you, brethren beloved by the Lord, because God from the beginning chose you for salvation through sanctification by the Spirit and belief in the truth (2 Thess. 2:13).

Sanctified by the Word of God

Sanctify them by Your truth. Your word is truth (John 17:17).

That He might sanctify and cleanse it with the washing of water by the word (Eph. 5:26).

Righteous Through Jesus Christ

Even the righteousness of God which is through faith in Jesus Christ to all and on all who believe. For there is no difference; for all have sinned and fall short of the glory of God (Romans 3:22,23).

And if Christ is in you, the body is dead because of sin, but the Spirit is life because of righteousness (Romans 8:10).

But of Him you are in Christ Jesus, who became for us wisdom from God — and righteousness and sanctification and redemption (1 Cor. 1:30).

For He made Him who knew no sin to be sin for us, that we might become the righteousness of God in Him (2 Cor. 5:21).

And that you put on the new man which was created according to God, in righteousness and true holiness (Eph. 4:24).

Being filled with the fruits of righteousness which are by Jesus Christ, to the glory and praise of God (Phil. 1:11).

Who Himself bore our sins in His own body on the tree, that we, having died to sins, might live for righteousness — by whose stripes you were healed (1 Peter 2:24).

The Holy Spirit

For the Holy Spirit will teach you in that very hour what you ought to say (Luke 12:12).

But the Helper, the Holy Spirit, whom the Father will send in My name, He will teach you all things, and bring to your remembrance all things that I said to you (John 14:26).

However, when He, the Spirit of truth, has come, He will guide you into all truth; for He will not speak on His own authority, but whatever He hears He will speak; and He will tell you things to come (John 16:13).

For as many as are led by the Spirit of God, these are sons of God (Romans 8:14).

The Spirit Himself bears witness with our spirit that we are children of God (Romans 8:16).

But God has revealed them to us through His Spirit. For the Spirit searches all things, yes, the deep things of God (1 Cor. 2:10).

For what man knows the things of a man except the spirit of the man which is in him? Even so no one knows the things of God except the Spirit of God (1 Cor. 2:11).

But if you are led by the Spirit, you are not under the law (Gal. 5:18).

The Holy Spirit Lives Inside a Believer

I will put My Spirit within you and cause you to walk in My statutes, and you will keep My judgments and do them (Ezek. 36:27).

Even the Spirit of truth, whom the world cannot receive, because it neither sees Him nor knows Him; but you know Him, for He dwells with you and will be in you (John 14:17).

Or do you not know that your body is the temple of the Holy Spirit who is in you, whom you have from God, and you are not your own? (1 Cor. 6:19).

And because you are sons, God has sent forth the Spirit of His Son into your hearts, crying out, "Abba, Father!" (Gal. 4:6).

That He would grant you, according to the riches of His glory, to be strengthened with might through His Spirit in the inner man (Eph. 3:16).

The Power of the Holy Spirit

But you shall receive power when the Holy Spirit has come upon you; and you shall be witnesses to Me in Jerusalem, and in all Judea and Samaria, and to the end of the earth (Acts 1:8).

And it shall come to pass in the last days, says God, That I will pour out of My Spirit on all flesh; your sons and your daughters shall prophesy, your young men shall see visions, your old men shall dream dreams (Acts 2:17).

And on My menservants and on My maidservants I will pour out My Spirit in those days; and they shall prophesy (Acts 2:18).

But if the Spirit of Him who raised Jesus from the dead dwells in you, He who raised Christ from the dead will also give life to your mortal bodies through His Spirit who dwells in you (Romans 8:11).

And such were some of you. But you were washed, but you were sanctified, but you were justified in the name of the Lord Jesus and by the Spirit of our God (1 Cor. 6:11).

For our gospel did not come to you in word only, but also in power, and in the Holy Spirit and in much assurance, as you know what kind of men we were among you for your sake (1 Thess. 1:5).

God also bearing witness both with signs and wonders, with various miracles, and gifts of the Holy Spirit, according to His own will? (Heb. 2:4).

The Integrity of God's Word

God is not a man, that He should lie, nor a son of man, that He should repent. Has He said, and will He not do it? Or has He spoken, and will He not make it good? (Num. 23:19).

Therefore know that the Lord your God, He is God, the faithful God who keeps covenant and mercy for a thousand generations with those who love Him and keep His commandments (Deut. 7:9).

The Lord of hosts has sworn, saying, "Surely, as I have thought, so it shall come to pass, and as I have purposed, so it shall stand" (Isaiah 14:24).

The grass withers, the flower fades, but the word of our God stands forever (Isaiah 40:8).

For He spoke, and it was done; He commanded, and it stood fast (Psalm 33:9).

My covenant I will not break, nor alter the word that has gone out of My lips (Psalm 89:34).

Forever, O Lord, Your word is settled in heaven (Psalm 119:89).

Every word of God is pure; He is a shield to those who put their trust in Him (Prov. 30:5).

For as the rain comes down, and the snow from heaven, and do not return there, but water the earth, and make it bring forth and bud, that it may give seed to the sower and bread to the eater, so shall My word be that goes forth from My mouth; it shall not return to Me void, but it shall accomplish what I please, and it shall prosper in the thing for which I sent it (Isaiah 55:10,11).

Heaven and earth will pass away, but My words will by no means pass away (Mark 13:31).

And being fully convinced that what He had promised He was also able to perform (Romans 4:21).

For all the promises of God in Him are Yes, and in Him Amen, to the glory of God through us (2 Cor. 1:20).

In hope of eternal life which God, who cannot lie, promised before time began (Titus 1:2).

That by two immutable things, in which it is impossible for God to lie, we might have strong consolation, who have fled for refuge to lay hold of the hope set before us (Heb. 6:18).

The Word of God in the Heart

I delight to do Your will, O my God, and Your law is within my heart (Psalm 40:8).

Your word I have hidden in my heart, that I might not sin against You (Psalm 119:11).

Incline my heart to Your testimonies, and not to covetousness (Psalm 119:36).

But this is the covenant that I will make with the house of Israel after those days, says the Lord: I will put My law in their minds, and write it on their hearts; and I will be their God, and they shall be My people (Jer. 31:33).

But what does it say? "The word is near you, even in your mouth and in your heart" (that is, the word of faith which we preach) (Romans 10:8).

Meditating on God's Word

This Book of the Law shall not depart from your mouth, but you shall meditate in it day and night, that you may observe to do according to all that is written in it. For then you will make your way prosperous, and then you will have good success (Joshua 1:8).

But his delight is in the law of the Lord, and in His law he meditates day and night (Psalm 1:2).

Let the words of my mouth and the meditation of my heart be acceptable in Your sight, O Lord, my strength and my redeemer (Psalm 19:14).

When I remember You on my bed, I meditate on You in the night watches (Psalm 63:6).

May my meditation be sweet to Him; I will be glad in the Lord (Psalm 104:34).

Oh, how I love Your law! It is my meditation all the day (Psalm 119:97).

My eyes are awake through the night watches, that I may meditate on Your word (Psalm 119:148).

The Cleansing of the Word of God

How can a young man cleanse his way? By taking heed according to Your word (Psalm 119:9).

Since you have purified your souls in obeying the truth through the Spirit in sincere love of the brethren, love one another fervently with a pure heart (1 Peter 1:22).

Therefore, having these promises, beloved, let us cleanse ourselves from all filthiness of the flesh and spirit, perfecting holiness in the fear of God (2 Cor. 7:1).

That He might sanctify and cleanse it with the washing of water by the word (Eph. 5:26).

The words of the Lord are pure words, like silver tried in a furnace of earth, purified seven times (Psalm 12:6).

The statutes of the Lord are right, rejoicing the heart; the commandment of the Lord is pure, enlightening the eyes (Psalm 19:8).

Seeking God

If My people who are called by My name will humble themselves, and pray and seek My face, and turn from their wicked ways, then I will hear from heaven, and will forgive their sin and heal their land (2 Chron. 7:14).

And those who know Your name will put their trust in You; for You, Lord, have not forsaken those who seek You (Psalm 9:10).

When You said, "Seek My face," my heart said to You, "Your face, Lord, I will seek" (Psalm 27:8).

But seek first the kingdom of God and His righteousness, and all these things shall be added to you (Matt. 6:33).

Ask, and it will be given to you; seek, and you will find; knock, and it will be opened to you. For everyone who asks receives, and he who seeks finds, and to him who knocks it will be opened (Matt. 7:7,8).

If then you were raised with Christ, seek those things which are above, where Christ is, sitting at the right hand of God (Col. 3:1).

Draw near to God and He will draw near to you. Cleanse your hands, you sinners; and purify your hearts, you double-minded (James 4:8).

Seek God Wholeheartedly

But from there you will seek the Lord your God, and you will find Him if you seek Him with all your heart and with all your soul (Deut. 4:29).

Blessed are those who keep His testimonies, who seek Him with the whole heart! (Psalm 119:2).

And you will seek Me and find Me, when you search for Me with all your heart (Jer. 29:13).

Prayer

Let us therefore come boldly to the throne of grace, that we may obtain mercy and find grace to help in time of need (Heb. 4:16).

If you then, being evil, know how to give good gifts to your children, how much more will your Father who is in heaven give good things to those who ask Him! (Matt. 7:11).

Praying in the Name of Jesus

Again I say to you that if two of you agree on earth concerning anything that they ask, it will be done for them by My Father in heaven. For where two or three are gathered together in My name, I am there in the midst of them (Matt. 18:19,20).

And whatever you ask in My name, that I will do, that the Father may be glorified in the Son (John 14:13).

If you ask anything in My name, I will do it (John 14:14).

You did not choose Me, but I chose you and appointed you that you should go and bear fruit, and that your fruit should remain, that whatever you ask the Father in My name He may give you (John 15:16).

And in that day you will ask Me nothing. Most assuredly, I say to you, whatever you ask the Father in My name He will give you (John 16:23).

Until now you have asked nothing in My name. Ask, and you will receive, that your joy may be full (John 16:24).

God Answers Prayer

"Am I a God near at hand," says the Lord, "and not a God afar off?" (Jer. 23:23).

But know that the Lord has set apart for Himself him who is godly; the Lord will hear when I call to Him (Psalm 4:3).

I waited patiently for the Lord; and He inclined to me, and heard my cry (Psalm 40:1).

Therefore I will look to the Lord; I will wait for the God of my salvation; my God will hear me (Micah 7:7).

Now this is the confidence that we have in Him, that if we ask anything according to His will, He hears us (1 John 5:14).

And if we know that He hears us, whatever we ask, we know that we have the petitions that we have asked of Him (1 John 5:15).

Hindrances to Prayer

If I regard iniquity in my heart, the Lord will not hear (Psalm 66:18).

Whoever shuts his ears to the cry of the poor will also cry himself and not be heard (Prov. 21:13).

One who turns away his ear from hearing the law, even his prayer shall be an abomination (Prov. 28:9).

Behold, the Lord's hand is not shortened, that it cannot save; nor His ear heavy, that it cannot hear. But your iniquities have separated you from your God; and your sins have hidden His face from you, so that He will not hear (Isaiah 59:1,2).

You lust and do not have. You murder and covet and cannot obtain. You fight and war. Yet you do not have because you do not ask (James 4:2).

You ask and do not receive, because you ask amiss, that you may spend it on your pleasures (James 4:3).

Likewise you husbands, dwell with them with understanding, giving honor to the wife, as to the weaker vessel, and as being heirs together of the grace of life, that your prayers may not be hindered (1 Peter 3:7).

For the eyes of the Lord are on the righteous, and his ears are open to their prayers; but the face of the Lord is against those who do evil (1 Peter 3:12).

Developing a Good Attitude

Lord, You have heard the desire of the humble; You will prepare their heart; You will cause Your ear to hear (Psalm 10:17).

Save me, O God! For the waters have come up to my neck (Psalm 69:1).

Though the Lord is on high, yet He regards the lowly; but the proud He knows from afar (Psalm 138:6).

The fear of the Lord is the instruction of wisdom, and before honor is humility (Prov. 15:33).

"For all those things My hand has made, and all those things exist," says the Lord. "But on this one will I look: on him who is poor and of a contrite spirit, and who trembles at My word" (Isaiah 66:2).

He has shown you, O man, what is good; and what does the Lord require of you but to do justly, to love mercy, and to walk humbly with your God? (Micah 6:8).

Blessed are the poor in spirit, for theirs is the kingdom of heaven (Matt. 5:3).

Yet it shall not be so among you; but whoever desires to become great among you, let him be your servant (Matt. 20:26).

And whoever exalts himself will be abased, and he who humbles himself will be exalted (Matt. 23:12).

Having then gifts differing according to the grace that is given to us, let us use them: if prophecy, let us prophesy in proportion to our faith (Romans 12:6).

But by the grace of God I am what I am, and His grace toward me was not in vain; but I labored more abundantly than they all, yet not I, but the grace of God which was with me (1 Cor. 15:10).

Humble yourselves in the sight of the Lord, and He will lift you up (James 4:10).

Therefore, as the elect of God, holy and beloved, put on tender mercies, kindness, humbleness of mind, meekness, longsuffering (Col. 3:12).

Therefore lay aside all filthiness and overflow of wickedness, and receive with meekness the implanted word, which is able to save your souls (James 1:21).

God Hates Pride

Though the Lord is on high, yet He regards the lowly; but the proud He knows from afar (Psalm 138:6).

The fear of the Lord is to hate evil; pride and arrogance and the evil way and the perverse mouth I hate (Prov. 8:13).

And He said to them, "You are those who justify yourselves before men, but God knows your hearts. For what is highly esteemed among men is an abomination in the sight of God" (Luke 16:15).

But He gives more grace. Therefore He says: "God resists the proud, but gives grace to the humble." Therefore submit to God. Resist the devil and he will flee from you (James 4:6,7).

Likewise you younger people, submit yourselves to your elders. Yes, all of you be submissive to one another, and be clothed with humility, for "God resists the proud, but gives grace to the humble" (1 Peter 5:5).

Controlling Anger

Cease from anger, and forsake wrath; do not fret — it only causes harm (Psalm 37:8).

He who is slow to wrath has great understanding, but he who is impulsive exalts folly (Prov. 14:29).

He who is slow to anger is better than the mighty, and he who rules his spirit than he who takes a city (Prov. 16:32).

Do not hasten in your spirit to be angry, for anger rests in the bosom of fools (Eccl. 7:9).

Let all bitterness, wrath, anger, clamor, and evil speaking be put away from you, with all malice (Eph. 4:31).

And be kind to one another, tenderhearted, forgiving one another, just as God in Christ also forgave you (Eph. 4:32).

But now you must also put off all these: anger, wrath, malice, blasphemy, filthy language out of your mouth (Col. 3:8).

Therefore, my beloved brethren, let every man be swift to hear, slow to speak, slow to wrath (James 1:19).

Love

The Lord opens the eyes of the blind; the Lord raises those who are bowed down; The Lord loves the righteous (Psalm 146:8).

The Lord has appeared of old to me, saying: "Yes, I have loved you with an everlasting love; therefore with lovingkindness I have drawn you" (Jer. 31:3).

And the glory which You gave Me I have given them, that they may be one just as We are one: I in them, and You in Me; that they may be made perfect in one, and that the world may know that You have sent Me, and have loved them as You have loved Me (John 17:22,23).

And I have declared to them Your name, and will declare it, that the love with which You loved Me may be in them, and I in them (John 17:26).

But God demonstrates His own love toward us, in that while we were still sinners, Christ died for us (Romans 5:8).

Hope

To them God willed to make known what are the riches of the glory of this mystery among the Gentiles: which is Christ in you, the hope of glory (Col. 1:27).

Now may our Lord Jesus Christ Himself, and our God and Father, who has loved us and given us everlasting consolation and good hope by grace (2 Thess. 2:16).

For in You, O Lord, I hope; You will hear, O Lord my God (Psalm 38:15).

Why are you cast down, O my soul? And why are you disquieted within me? Hope in God, for I shall yet praise Him for the help of His countenance (Psalm 42:5).

But I will hope continually, and will praise You yet more and more (Psalm 71:14).

O Israel, hope in the Lord; for with the Lord there is mercy, and with Him is abundant redemption (Psalm 130:7).

Happy is he who has the God of Jacob for his help, whose hope is in the Lord his God (Psalm 146:5).

Joy

You will show me the path of life; in Your presence is fullness of joy; at Your right hand are pleasures forevermore (Psalm 16:11).

So the ransomed of the Lord shall return, and come to Zion with singing, with everlasting joy on their heads; they shall obtain joy and gladness, and sorrow and sighing shall flee away (Isaiah 51:11).

For you shall go out with joy, and be led out with peace; the mountains and the hills shall break forth into singing before you, and all the trees of the field shall clap their hands (Isaiah 55:12).

And you will have joy and gladness, and many will rejoice at his birth (Luke 1:14).

These things I have spoken to you, that My joy may remain in you, and that your joy may be full (John 15:11).

And the disciples were filled with joy and with the Holy Spirit (Acts 13:52).

For the kingdom of God is not food and drink, but righteousness and peace and joy in the Holy Spirit (Romans 14:17).

Now may the God of hope fill you with all joy and peace in believing, that you may abound in hope by the power of the Holy Spirit (Romans 15:13).

Mercy

All the paths of the Lord are mercy and truth, to such as keep His covenant and His testimonies (Psalm 25:10).

Many sorrows shall be to the wicked; but he who trusts in the Lord, mercy shall surround him (Psalm 32:10).

Your mercy, O Lord, is in the heavens, and Your faithfulness reaches to the clouds (Psalm 36:5).

The Lord is merciful and gracious, slow to anger, and abounding in mercy (Psalm 103:8).

Let the wicked forsake his way, and the unrighteous man his thoughts; let him return to the Lord, and He will have mercy on him; and to our God, for He will abundantly pardon (Isaiah 55:7).

But God, who is rich in mercy, because of His great love with which He loved us (Eph. 2:4).

Not by works of righteousness which we have done, but according to His mercy He saved us, through the washing of regeneration and renewing of the Holy Spirit (Titus 3:5).

Let us therefore come boldly to the throne of grace, that we may obtain mercy and find grace to help in time of need (Heb. 4:16).

Peace

And by Him to reconcile all things to Himself, by Him, whether things on earth or things in heaven, having made peace through the blood of His cross (Col. 1:20).

Blessed is the man who walks not in the counsel of the ungodly, nor stands in the path of sinners, nor sits in the seat of the scornful (Psalm 1:1).

For it is not an enemy who reproaches me; then I could bear it. Nor is it one who hates me who has magnified himself against me; then I could hide from him (Psalm 55:12).

Now I beg you, brethren, through the Lord Jesus Christ, and through the love of the Spirit, that you strive together with me in your prayers to God for me (Romans 15:30).

And let the peace of God rule in your hearts, to which also you were called in one body; and be thankful (Col. 3:15).

Now may the Lord of peace Himself give you peace always in every way. The Lord be with you all (2 Thess. 3:16).

But now in Christ Jesus you who once were far off have been made near by the blood of Christ (Eph. 2:13).

For He Himself is our peace, who has made both one, and has broken down the middle wall of division between us (Eph. 2:14).

Therefore, having been justified by faith, we have peace with God through our Lord Jesus Christ (Romans 5:1).

Peace I leave with you, My peace I give to you; not as the world gives do I give to you. Let not your heart be troubled, neither let it be afraid (John 14:27).

These things I have spoken to you, that in Me you may have peace. In the world you will have tribulation; but be of good cheer, I have overcome the world (John 16:33).

Comfort

I, even I, am He who comforts you. Who are you that you should be afraid of a man who will die, and of the son of a man who will be made like grass? (Isaiah 51:12).

But the Helper, the Holy Spirit, whom the Father will send in My name, He will teach you all things, and bring to your remembrance all things that I said to you (John 14:26).

Blessed be the God and Father of our Lord Jesus Christ, the Father of mercies and God of all comfort, who comforts us in all our tribulation, that we may be able to comfort those who are in any trouble, with the comfort with which we ourselves are comforted by God (2 Cor. 1:3,4).

Eternal Life

For God so loved the world that He gave His only begotten Son, that whoever believes in Him should not perish but have everlasting life (John 3:16).

But whoever drinks of the water that I shall give him will never thirst. But the water that I shall give him will become in him a fountain of water springing up into everlasting life (John 4:14).

Most assuredly, I say to you, he who hears My word and believes in Him who sent Me has everlasting life, and shall not come into judgment, but has passed from death into life (John 5:24).

Most assuredly, I say to you, he who believes in Me has everlasting life (John 6:47).

My sheep hear My voice, and I know them, and they follow Me. And I give them eternal life, and they shall never perish; neither shall anyone snatch them out of My hand (John 10:27,28).

8

The Greatest Book in the World

The Bible is the greatest book in the whole world. Its pages are filled with life. Because its words were breathed by the Holy Spirit, its message is deathless, its commands changeless, and its truth timeless. Jesus, who is our Life, pledges His personal presence in His Word. He Himself said, "The words that I speak to you are spirit, and they are life" (John 6:63).

The Bible is a book for all occasions. The brokenhearted find solace as they meditate on it, and the thirsty drink in the water of life. The hungry soul satisfies himself, and the questioner discovers the solution to his problem. The bereaved and the comfortless sense His everlasting arms surrounding them. The weak discover strength, and the poor partake of the unsearchable riches in Christ.

Sages must lay aside their earthly wisdom at the feet of the Word of God to apprehend its true wisdom and knowledge. The troubled soul finds peace that passes all understanding, and the suicidal embrace the Prince of Life within its pages.

The sick find the Great Physician, the Son of righteousness rising with healing in His wings. The lonely discover in its pages a Friend at all times. The widow finds her Husband, and the orphan finds the Father of the fatherless.

The depressed soul discovers in its commandments joy unspeakable, and the bound realize the truth that sets them free. The outcast finds a city of refuge, and the unloved meet the God of love. The politician beholds the Desire of all nations in its constitution, and the unlearned receives the knowledge of the Holy.

We stand defenseless against the attack of the enemy of our soul, but the Word in our hands becomes the Flaming Sword of the Spirit that is sharper than any two-edged sword. It goes in every direction to pierce the power of darkness.

Its truth purifies the soul; its statutes gladden the heart; its law converts the soul; its testimony imparts wisdom; and its command enlightens the eyes.

The Book of Love

It is a book of love written by God to a sinful world. It is the revelation of God to man and contains the plan of salvation. It is our guide to knowing our Lord and Savior Jesus Christ. It is the legacy that Jesus Christ bequeaths to the Church. Its promises are true; its doctrine infallible and inerrant; its warnings to be taken seriously.

It has been the court of appeal throughout the history of God's people. Every doctrine and conduct must rise or fall before it. It is the judge of heresies and the justifier of sound doctrine.

It will remain throughout eternity, even when heaven and earth cease to exist. Its message will continue shining with a divine glow, bubbling with divine energy and pulsating with the life of its Author — Almighty God.

The Word of God is the miracle drug for every ailment. It is the antidote to our emotional disorder. No anti-depressant approaches its effectiveness. Other drugs may have dangerous side effects, but the Word of God has none. It is whole. It is safe. It is perfect. It proceeds from the God who made us. It is therefore compatible with your heart. When the Word heals, no residue of the past remains.

It is medicine to our spirit. Our inner man is vibrant, healthy, and buoyant because of its medicinal properties. It convicts us of sin, and it examines our motives. It reveals to us our very thoughts, and we are laid bare before its searching light. Yet it binds our sick soul and applies the balm of Gilead to it. Blessings accrue for all who diligently search its pages and follow its prescription.

What more can we say about this Book? It is the Book of the ages, the Book of power, and the Book of love. It remains invincible against all the attacks of the enemy. Its authority cannot be set aside, and its message cannot be outdated.

In keeping it, we are blessed. In hiding it in our hearts, we keep ourselves from sinning against a holy God. In searching it, we receive eternal life. In loving it, we obtain peace. In heeding it, our ways are cleansed. In imbibing its truth, we are set free. In submitting to its authority, we are safe. In eating it, our hearts experience the joy of the Holy Spirit.

Oh, that men would take refuge in the written Word of God! Read it to be wise. Read it to be enlightened in the true knowledge of God. Read it again and again. Chew on it, feast on it, dine on it, and you will discover the meaning of life — life in all its abundance.

9

A Word to Unbelievers

If you are not a born again child of God, all that you have read will mean little to you. The benefits of Scripture memorization are only for those who are born again.

If you haven't invited Jesus Christ into your heart, the Holy Spirit doesn't dwell inside you to teach you the Scriptures and to impress its truth in your heart.

You may know the Bible and be able to quote it verbatim. But for the Word to do you any good, it must be in your spirit. Only a spirit that is alive to God can enjoy the privileges of the Word of God. If you are not born again, you can yield your life to Christ today.

Your eternity is at stake. When you die, you will have to spend eternity in heaven or in the lake of fire. Your response to the Son of God determines your destiny. Can you afford to take the risk of not settling this issue? Is it worth it?

Can you remember a particular time when you invited Jesus into your life? Did you receive the assurance that He came in? This new birth cannot be inherited. Your parents being religious or holding a high position in the church does not guarantee you a place in heaven. The decision must be yours alone.

If you have not given your life to Christ, this is the time to do it. Do not wait until tomorrow, for you do not know what tomorrow holds. Those who will die tomorrow in an accident or next year from disease are unaware of their impending death. What makes you sure that you are not in that number? Life is uncertain. For your own sake, you need to know what God has to tell you through the Scriptures.

God's Remedy for Sin

You have sinned against a holy God. "For all have sinned and fall short of the glory of God" (Romans 3:23). The holiness of God demands that you pay for your sin. "The soul that sinneth, it shall die" (Ezek. 18:4, KJV). Although you enjoy physical life, you are dead spiritually. This spiritual death, into which we are all born as a result of Adam's sin, eventually leads to eternal death — spending eternity in the lake of fire.

God saw our condition and, in His mercy and love, intervened. He sent His only Son, Jesus Christ, to take away our sin and to die the death that we deserved. He became the Lamb of God who took away the sin of the world. He was born into our world to die. That was His primary mission. The Son of God had to clothe himself in human flesh in order to defeat the devil — the author of sin, death, and human suffering.

As Jesus hung on the cross at Calvary, He shed His blood, which is the only means by which your sins can be wiped away

— never to be remembered again by God. The cross of Christ became the bridge between God and man. There was no other way to reconcile sinners to a holy God. No man could do this. Being a sinner, not even a prophet could shed his blood for mankind. The only one qualified to shed His blood was the sinless Son of God. What great love God had for man!

On the third day, the Father raised Jesus from the dead. His death atoned or compensated for your sins, and His resurrection justified you, or put you in right standing before God.

Your Response

What is your response to God's divine plan? You must turn away from your sins — both small and great — for they are all grievous to God. Lying, having sex outside of marriage, taking drugs, backbiting, consulting evil spirits, disobeying parents, thinking evil thoughts, and stealing are some common sins. You know your sins, and so does God.

Find a quiet place where you can examine your heart. As God brings particular sins to mind, confess them to Him. Tell Him you are sorry. Mean it and decide to live in a new way that pleases God. That's true repentance.

Next, ask Him to forgive you and to cleanse you by the blood of Jesus. Believe that He has done just what He said. "If we confess our sins, He is faithful and just to forgive us our sins and to cleanse us from all unrighteousness" (1 John 1:9). Jesus will not reject you because of your sins. No sin is too black; no sin is so terrible that it cannot be wiped away. The blood of Jesus wipes away all sin, both great and small.

Even if you have handed your soul over to the devil, the blood of Jesus can cleanse and deliver you. Listen to the promise of God to all who dare to repent: "Though your sins be as scarlet, they shall be as white as snow; though they be red like crimson, they shall be as wool" (Isaiah 1:18, KJV).

Third, ask Christ to come into your heart. He has promised, "Behold, I stand at the door, and knock. If anyone hears My voice and opens the door, I will come in to him . . ." (Rev. 3:20).

Then you must confess aloud that Jesus is Lord and that God raised Him from the dead. Pray this prayer:

> Dear God, I confess my sins to You, and I repent of them (Tell Him all the sins you can remember). I ask You to forgive me of all my sins — the ones I remember and the ones I don't — through the blood of Jesus. I invite Jesus Christ into my heart. I confess Him as Lord, and I also believe with my heart that You raised Him from the dead for my justification. I believe that my sins are forgiven. I believe that Jesus Christ has come into my heart. I believe that I have been justified. I believe that I am saved, and I have become a child of God. Thank You, Father. In Jesus' name. Amen.

Your New Life

Jesus is faithful to His Word. He is not a man who lies. If you sincerely ask Him to come to your heart, He will. He is eager to give you a new start and a zest for living. You will experience a life that you never dreamed possible.

Now, thank Him and share your newfound joy with a friend. Find a Bible-believing church. God will direct you to a good church if you ask Him. Spend time with other Christians to encourage you in your relationship with God. You should also read the Bible and pray everyday.

Finally, begin memorizing and meditating on the Word of God. You will not be the only one who notices the amazing transformation in your life.

OTHER BOOKS FROM
Pneuma Life Publishing

Why?
by T.D. Jakes

Why do the righteous, who have committed their entire lives to obeying God, seem to endure so much pain and experience such conflict? These perplexing questions have plagued and bewildered Christians for ages. In this anointed and inspirational new book, Bishop T.D. Jakes, provocatively and skillfully answers these questions and many more as well as answering the "Why" of the anointed. *Also available as a workbook*

Water in the Wilderness
by T.D. Jakes

Just before you apprehend your greatest conquest, expect the greatest struggle. Many are perplexed who encounter this season of adversity. This book will show you how to survive the worst of times with the greatest of ease, and will cause fountains of living waters to spring out of the parched, sun—drenched areas in your life. This word is a refreshing stream in the desert for the weary traveler.

The Harvest
by T.D. Jakes

Have you been sidetracked by Satan? Are you preoccupied with the things of this world? Are you distracted by one crisis after another? You need to get your act together before it's too late! God's strategy for the end-time harvest is already set in motion. Phase One is underway, and Phase Two is close behind. If you don't want to be left out tomorrow, you need to take action today. With startling insight, T.D. Jakes sets the record straight. You'll be shocked to learn how God is separating people into two distinct categories. One thing is certain – after reading *The Harvest,* you'll know exactly where you stand with God. This book will help you discover who will and who won't be included in the final ingathering and determine what it takes to be prepared. If you miss *The Harvest,* you'll regret it for all eternity!

Help Me! I've Fallen
by T.D. Jakes

"Help! I've fallen, and I can't get up." This cry, made popular by a familiar television commercial, points out the problem faced by many Christians today. Have you ever stumbled and fallen with no hope of getting up? Have you been wounded and hurt by others? Are you so far down you think you'll never stand again? Don't despair. All Christians fall from time to time. Life knocks us off balance, making it hard – if not impossible – to get back on our feet. The cause of the fall is not as important as what we do while we're down. T.D. Jakes explains how – and Whom – to ask for help. In a struggle to regain your balance, this book is going to be your manual to recovery! Don't panic. This is just a test!

The God Factor
by James Giles
Is something missing in your life? Do you find yourself at the mercy of your circumstances? Is your self-esteem at an all-time low? Are your dreams only a faded memory? You could be missing the one element that could make the difference between success and failure, poverty and prosperity, and creativity and apathy. Knowing God supplies the creative genius you need to reach your potential and realize your dream. You'll be challenged as James Giles shows you how to tap into your God-given genius; take steps toward reaching your goal; pray big and get answers; eat right and stay healthy; prosper economically and personally; and leave a lasting legacy for your children.

Making the Most of Your Teenage Years
by David Burrows
Most teenagers live for today. Living only for today, however, can kill you. When teenagers have no plan for their future, they follow a plan that someone else devised. Unfortunately, this plan often leads them to drugs, sex, crime, jail, and an early death. How can you make the most of your teenage years? Discover who you really are – and how to plan for the three phases of your life. You develop your skill, achieve your dreams, and still have fun.

The Biblical Principles of Success
Arthur L. Mackey Jr.
There are only three types of people in the world: 1. People who make things happen; 2. People who watch things happen; and 3. People who do not know what in the world is happening. *The Biblical Principles of Success,* will help you become one who makes things happen. Success is not a matter of "doing it my way." It is turning from a personal, selfish philosophy to God's outreaching, sharing way of life. This powerful book teaches you how to tap into success principles that are guaranteed – *the Biblical principles of success!*

The Flaming Sword
by Tai Ikomi
Scripture memorization and meditation bring tremendous spiritual power, however many Christians find it to be an uphill task. Committing Scriptures to memory will transform the mediocre Christian to a spiritual giant. This book will help you to become addicted to the powerful practice of Scripture memorization and help you obtain the victory that you desire in every area of your life. *The Flaming Sword* is your pathway to spiritual growth and a more intimate relationship with God.

This is My Story
by Candi Staton
This is My Story is a touching autobiography about a gifted young child who rose from obscurity and poverty to stardom and wealth. With a music career that included selling millions of albums and topping the charts came a life of brokenness, loneliness, and despair. This book will make you cry and laugh as you witness one woman's search for success and love.

Another Look at Sex
by Charles Phillips
This book is undoubtedly a head turner and eye opener that will cause you to take another close look at sex. In this book, Charles Phillips openly addresses this seldom discussed subject and gives life-changing advice on sex to married couples and singles. If you have questions about sex, this is the book for you.

Four Laws of Productivity
by Dr. Mensa Otabil
Success has no favorites, but it does have associates. Success will come to anyone who will pay the price to receive its benefits. *Four Laws of Productivity* will give you the powerful keys that will help you achieve your life's goals. You will learn how to discover God's gift in you, develop your gift, perfect your gift, and utilize your gift to its maximum potential. The principles revealed in this timely book will radically change your life.

Single Life
by Earl D. Johnson
A book that candidly addresses the spiritual and physical dimensions of the single life is finally here. *Single Life* shows the reader how to make their singleness a celebration rather than a burden. This positive approach to singles uses enlightening examples from Apostle Paul, himself a single, to beautifully portray the dynamic aspects of the single life

by serving the Lord more effectively. The book gives fresh insight on practical issues such as coping with sexual desires, loneliness, and preparation for your future mate. Written in a lively style, the author admonishes singles to seek first the kingdom of God and rest assured in God's promise to supply their needs... including a life partner!

Strategies for Saving the Next Generation

by Dave Burrows

This book will teach you how to start and effectively operate a vibrant youth ministry. This book is filled with practical tips and insight gained over a number of years working with young people from the street to the parks to the church. Dave Burrows offers the reader vital information that will produce results if carefully considered and adapted. Excellent for pastors and youth pastors as well as youth workers and those involved with youth ministry.

The Call of God

by Jefferson Edwards

Since I have been called to preach, now what? Many sincere Christians are confused about their call to the ministry. Some are zealous and run ahead of their time and season of training and preparation while others are behind their time neglecting the gift of God within them. *The Call of God* gives practical instruction for pastors and leaders to refine and further develop their ministry and tips on how to nourish and develop others with God's call to effectively proclaim the gospel of Christ. *The Call of God* will help you to • Have clarity from God as to what ministry involves • Be able to identify and affirm the call in your life • See what stage you are in your call from God • Remove confusion in relation to the processing of a call or the making of the person • Understand the development of the anointing to fulfill your call.

Come, Let Us Pray

by Emmette Weir

Are you satisfied with your prayer life? Are you finding that your prayers are often dull, repetitive and lacking in spiritual power? Are you looking for ways to improve your relationship with God? Would you like to be able to pray more effectively? Then *Come, Let Us Pray* will help you in these areas and more. If you want to gain the maximum spiritual experience from your prayer life and enter into the very presence of God – *Come, Let Us Pray.*

Leadership in the New Testament Church
by Earl D. Johnson
Leadership in the New Testament Church offers practical and applicable insight into the role of leadership in the present day church. In this book, the author explains the qualities that leaders must have, explores the interpersonal relationships between the leader and his staff, the leaders' influence in the church and society and how to handle conflicts that arise among leaders.

Becoming A Leader
by Myles Munroe
Many consider leadership to be no more than staying ahead of the pack, but that is a far cry from what leadership is. Leadership is deploying others to become as good as or better than you are. Within each of us lies the potential to be an effective leader. *Becoming A Leader* uncovers the secrets of dynamic leadership that will show you how to be a leader in your family, school, community, church and job. No matter where you are or what you do in life this book can help you to inevitably become a leader. Remember: it is never too late to become a leader. As in every tree there is a forest, so in every follower there is a leader.

Becoming A Leader Workbook
by Myles Munroe
Now you can activate your leadership potential through the *Becoming A Leader Workbook*. This workbook has been designed to take you step by step through the leadership principles taught in *Becoming A Leader*. As you participate in the work studies in this workbook you will see the true leader inside you develop and grow into maturity. *"Knowledge with action produces results."*

Mobilizing Human Resources
by Richard Pinder
Pastor Pinder gives an in-depth look at how to organize, motivate, and deploy members of the Body of Christ in a manner that produces maximum effect for your ministry. This book will assist you in organizing and motivating your troops for effective and efficient ministry. It will also help the individual believer in recognizing their place in the body, using their God given abilities and talents to maximum effect.

The Minister's Topical Bible
by Derwin Stewart
The Minister's Topical Bible covers every aspect of the ministry providing quick and easy access to scriptures in a variety of ministry related topics. This handy reference tool can be effectively used in

leadership training, counseling, teaching, sermon preparation, and personal study.

The Believer's Topical Bible

by Derwin Stewart

The Believer's Topical Bible covers every aspect of a Christian's relationship with God and man, providing biblical answers and solutions for all challenges. It is a quick, convenient, and thorough reference Bible that has been designed for use in personal devotions and group Bible studies. With over 3,500 verses systematically organized under 240 topics, it is the largest devotional-topical Bible available in the New International Version and the King James Version.

The Layman's Guide to Counseling

by Susan Wallace

The increasing need for counseling has caused today's Christian leaders to become more sensitive to raise up lay-counselors to share this burden with them. Jesus' command is to "set the captives free." *The Layman's Guide to Counseling* shows you how. A number of visual aids in the form of charts, lists, and tables are also integrated into this reference book: the most comprehensive counseling tool available. *The Layman's Guide to Counseling* gives you the knowledge you need to use advanced principles of Word-based counseling to equip you to be effective in your counseling ministry. **Topics Include** • Inner Healing • Parenting • Marriage • Deliverance • Abuse • Forgiveness • Drug & Alcohol Recovery • Youth Counseling • Holy Spirit • Premarital Counseling

Available at your local bookstore or by contacting:

Pneuma Life Publishing
P.O. Box 10612
Bakersfield, CA 93389-0612

1-800-727-3218
1-805-324-1741